G000166798

"There have been numerous respc
which have been as philosophically
'new atheism' itself. But this book
mere negative apologetic against th
the book dealing with the issues of
the reader to the centrality of the
reason the book is much more than a mere exercise in pure g

This book displays an engagement with contemporary culture but not in a way that 'dumbs down' the content of the argument for theism and the specifics of Christian belief. On the contrary, the engagement with contemporary culture is used by the author to illuminate and explicate some difficult philosophical and theological issues and this means that it is a book that is ideal for younger readers and those unfamiliar with philosophy and theology – it is in fact an excellent introduction to both in addition to its sophisticated and positive case for the rationality of Christian belief."

Patrick J. Roche
Tutor in Philosophy of Religion, Irish Baptist College Moira,
Northern Ireland

'New Atheism: A Survival Guide' starts with a look at what the author calls the 'sneer pressure' which comes both from some of the 'new atheists' and from atheist blogs and websites. Graham Veale looks critically at some of atheism's sneers, and suggests that perhaps a little more thought (and even a little more courtesy!) might be appropriate on their part. He makes a concise, positive, case for theism, and suggests that perhaps atheism isn't so obviously true after all. If you are a Christian who has been sneered at, or an atheist who sneers, then you should think about reading this book, and while you read it – think!

Mark McCartney
Senior Lecturer in Mathematics, University of Ulster
Co-editor Kelvin: Life, Labours and Legacy,
Londonderry, Northern Ireland

This is a great wee book which is an excellent introduction to and summary of, the current controversy surrounding the New Atheism. Graham Veale does a superb job in outlining the main issues and providing an excellent resource for those who want to understand what it is all about and how to respond. Highly recommended!

David Robertson
Pastor of St Peter's Free Churcn, Dundee
Author of *The Dawkins Letters*

With insightful illustrations and a highly readable style, this book provides a superb response to the New Atheism's objections to belief in God and the Christian faith. It achieves this by drawing on some of the best Christian scholarship available and presenting it in an introductory and accessible way. For students whose faith is under attack, this is the survival guide you need.

DAVID GLASS
Author of *Atheism's New Clothes.*

In a radio conversation I suggested to Richard Dawkins that his simplistic rhetoric generated more heat than light. Dawkins agreed and Graham Veale shows why. In measured tones and sharp logic, Veale cuts through the verbal nonsense that obscures the truth. He demonstrates that the Christian faith is reasonable and stands up to scrutiny while much of the new atheist case relies on noise and bluster. The emperor's new clothes turned out to be an illusion and this excellent volume reveals Richard Dawkins' arguments to also be embarrassingly thin!

CHRIS SINKINSON
Lecturer in Old Testament and Apologetics
Moorlands College

With common sense and uncommon clarity, Graham Veale surveys the popular arguments of the New Atheists that have given so many people intellectual indigestion. Wondering what to do with refried Hume? Need to slay a spaghetti monster? Grab this book – and pass the parmesan!

TIMOTHY MCGREW
Professor of Philosophy
Western Michigan University

New Atheism

A Survival Guide

Graham Veale

CHRISTIAN
FOCUS

Graham Veale is head of religious education at City of Armagh High School, where he's taught for the last fifteen years. He has a theology degree from Queen's University, Belfast through the Irish Baptist College. Currently, he's pursuing postgraduate studies at Queens (for an MTh). He is also co-founder of *Saints and Sceptics* (with Dr David Glass) a Northern Irish apologetics organization. (www. saintsandsceptics.org)

Copyright © Graham Veale

paperback ISBN 978-1-78191-316-1
epub ISBN 978-1-78191-392-5
Mobi ISBN 978-1-78191-394-9

10 9 8 7 6 5 4 3 2 1

Published in 2013
by
Christian Focus Publications,
Geanies House, Fearn, Ross-shire,
IV20 1TW, Scotland, Great Britain

www.christianfocus.com

Cover design by
Daniel van Straaten

Printed by
Bell and Bain, Glasgow

MIX
Paper from
responsible sources
FSC® C007785

Contents

Acknowledgements

Patrick Roche, Mark McCartney, Peter Morrow and David Glass persisted in their support for this little book. They had more faith in me that I did, and I would like to thank them for their encouragement, intelligence and wisdom. David not only offered me ideas and guidance; he and I have a friendship, founded on a love of evangelism and apologetics, which now spans over twenty years. Peter has a pastor's heart and mind; his counsel is always welcome. I would also like to thank the Rev. Paul Ritchie for reading some early drafts of some early chapters, and telling me that I should continue with my writing. The team at Christian Focus Publications have been wonderful; I would especially like to thank Philip Ross for his dedication and discernment.

I will always aspire to the enduring faith and Christian character of my father, Harry. His knowledge, insight and compassion have been essential to my walk with the Lord. My mum, Elizabeth, has taught me that a little kindness will mean more to children than a hundred books or a thousand educational initiatives. If I have achieved anything as a teacher it is to my parent's credit. My father-in-law, the Rev. Roy Hamilton, has a razor sharp mind and insists that Christians put good sense above academic abstractions. Nicola is both long-suffering enough to have married me and to have guided me through a surprisingly long writing project. I could not achieve much of anything without her.

Finally, I would like to thank Kenneth Crooks and Andrew Turkington for the outstanding leadership they gave to City of Armagh High School. The school has been at the centre of my family's life for over fifteen years; yet parents, carers, staff and pupils keep teaching me something new every day. The spirit of a community cannot be quantified; therefore it is rarely valued, or even recognised, by politicians, boards of education or inspectorates. With that in mind, this book is dedicated to all those who built the community of City of Armagh High School.

Preface

When Atheism Went Viral

Educators are beginning to realize that the information age might not be the friend of thought. We have created a culture in which students expect to find the answers to life's deepest questions on 'Google'. Meanwhile, school curricula are strong on teaching technical skills and personal values, but say nothing about wisdom and virtue. As a result students do not engage in, and do not see the need for, rational discourse. They become dogmatists, who can only assert their fundamental beliefs, and who never take the time to convince anyone of anything. They can only attempt to intimidate or browbeat assent into the minds of the unconverted.

This mentality is not the preserve of the religious; in fact, it is most clearly epitomized by the ignorant screeds of New Atheism. To illustrate, Richard Dawkins has suggested that his fellow New Atheists should

> '...go beyond humorous ridicule, sharpen our barbs to a point where they really hurt...I think we should probably abandon the irremediably religious precisely because that is what they are—irremediable. I am more interested in the fence-sitters who haven't really considered the question

very long or very carefully. And I think that they are likely to be swayed by a display of naked contempt. Nobody likes to be laughed at. Nobody wants to be the butt of contempt.'[1]

This typifies a fundamentalist attitude. There is no attempt to engage with serious critiques of atheism. Dawkins simply assumes that unbelief is infinitely superior to Christian superstition, and demands that his audience share his blind faith. This should lead us to ask how a prominent academic can make a public virtue out of his own invincible ignorance.

Perhaps this is the oddest feature of New Atheism: its tendency to be shaped by the forces it so implacably opposes. New Atheist literature found a wide readership in the wake of 9/11 because it offered a radical response to the violence of fundamentalist Islamism. However, in a panicked response to the dangers of religious violence, New Atheism forced false dichotomies on the reader. You can *either* have religion *or* rationality; you can *either* be devout, *or* you can be tolerant.

But the simple fact is that our liberties grew out of Christian morality. Philosophers and historians have noted the importance of Christian thought for the very concept of human rights. Christian theologians like Tertullian and Chrysostom were arguing for religious tolerance centuries before the Enlightenment. Lactantius, for example, argued:

> '...if you wish to defend religion by bloodshed, and by tortures, and by guilt, it will no longer be defended, but will be polluted and profaned. For nothing is so much a matter of free-will as religion; in which, if the mind of the worshipper is disinclined to it, religion is at once taken away, and ceases to exist.'[2]

---

[1] Richard Dawkins open-minded comments can be read richarddawkins.net/ articles/3767-truckling-to-the-faithful-a-spoonful-of-jesus-helps-darwin-go-down/comments?page=1#comment_351636 (retrieved July 21 2012).

[2] For further reading on the roots of tolerance see www.saintsandsceptics. org/the-roots-of-tolerance-and-reason/

Furthermore, Christianity does not depend on blind faith. The Apostle Paul presented rational critiques of paganism in Lystra, Athens, and in his letter to the Romans. Philosophers from Anselm and Aquinas to Plantinga and Swinburne have presented robust arguments for the Christian faith. Even preachers, like Edwards, Wesley and Chalmers, wrote detailed defenses of their beliefs. Christians have always sought to give a reasoned answer for the hope that is within them. The New Atheist is welcome to disagree with centuries of Christian scholarship; but only a blind, prejudiced dogmatism could pretend that it does not exist!

Sound-bite Scepticism

Yet few consumers are interested in mature thought and calm reflection. Media savvy atheists have learned to target their message at a younger, more cynical, market. Their aim is to sell consumers a sense of intellectual superiority for a low intellectual price. The New Atheists have proven that such scepticism sells. Their books require no knowledge of, or interest in, history or philosophy, or even science. Anecdotal evidence and quips replace sound arguments.

These products are easy to read, easy to quote and easy to retail. In Britain, Dawkins' 'The God Delusion'[3] was endorsed on the dust jacket by Phillip Pullman (a children's author) and Derren Brown (an illusionist). Celebrity endorsements were preferred to favourable academic reviews. This tells us something about the merchandise and its market. Given that the 'New Atheists' have contributed less substance than style.

Meanwhile, online communities have provided many atheists with a new sense of identity and purpose. Until recently sceptics had no alternative to the Church. The internet has changed all that; an impressive number of blogs and forums

---

[3] All quotations from *The God Delusion* are taken from the 2006 revised and updated paperback edition, published by Black-Swan.

have filled the Church shaped hole in the young atheist's life. Forums and chat-rooms are oddly addictive, and drag people back daily to exchange ideas and comments. Thanks to sites like 'The Richard Dawkins Forum' the individual atheist no longer feels isolated; he is part of a vibrant, well-educated and technologically literate community.

The 2010 controversy over the future of the Richard Dawkins Forum illustrates the power of online communities. In March 2010 Richard Dawkins decided to restructure the discussion boards at the Richard Dawkins' Forum. For reasons that will remain unclear to outsiders this was a deeply unpopular decision, and it provoked extremely angry, sometimes vulgar, comments on several message boards. Dawkins attempted to put a lid on the row by temporarily locking down his board.

But if Dawkins fought the net, then the net won. He simply underestimated the sense of identity that young atheists gain by interacting with each other on his forum. Online the reaction to his comments was furious, and Dawkins was eventually forced to apologise:

> The RDF forum was an envigorating and intellectually stimulating experience for me, a home away from home where I could be with like-minded folks in a warmly welcoming, receptive, and cordial atmosphere. Its membership formed a great community, one that shared the joys of new friendships and marriages and the pangs of deaths and losses, while providing a place where atheists stuck in the closet in some religious wilderness could feel safe and wecome. Thousands of members were of this kind.

> To Prof. R. Dawkins: please imagine that YOU, as an obscure person who does not make lots of money from book deals and speaking engagements, put many hours of work and one's heart and soul into building and maintaining something because you believed in it with all your heart.

> If you have a real community on your board, including many activists helping to advance your cause, do not treat them like chattels or serfs...[4]

Other blogs, like PZ Myer's '*Pharyngula*' or Jerry Coyne's '*Why Evolution is True*', are beautifully tailored for a large audience. To maintain a blog you must constantly post new comments. Little reflection is needed as there is no editorial process. In any case the more time a blogger spends in preparation, the lower his output will be. The most popular comments are brief, snappy and witty. The most outrageous posts gain the most attention. There are honourable exceptions—but, in the main, blogs are intellectual junk foods. They're fun and addictive, but they provide little for the mind to chew on.

You will not find informed critiques of Christianity on these blogs; you will find that New Atheism can be dumbed-down even further. Clichés, caricatures, and witticisms dominate proceedings. For example, '*Pharyngula*' is a clumsy and ignorant attack on religion; indeed, that is the whole *point* of this blog. It takes a great deal of intelligence and effort to be so ill-informed. To Myers, religious belief is only worthy of contempt, so he will not study it seriously. His aim is to debase and sully Christianity. Why carefully research the grounds and justification for religious belief when you can steal and desecrate consecrated wafers from a Roman Catholic Mass?

As propaganda New Atheist websites are exceptionally effective. To some extent, this is merely an effect of the modern cult of expertise. Coyne, Myers and Dawkins are obviously very intelligent men, and experts in their fields. Their readers make the lazy assumption that this expertise gives these writers authority to pronounce on religion, philosophy and ethics.

---

[4] The responses from his fans were retrieved from rationalia.com/forum/viewtopic.php?f=75&t=9279&start=45 (retrieved 30th Dec 2011) and heathen-hub.com/blog.php?b=242 (retrieved 30th Dec 2011).

However, an expert loses his right to make such judgments when he makes no effort to integrate his knowledge with other fields of learning. New atheists refuse to make the effort, or to acquire the humility, to achieve such understanding and wisdom.

This is a book for readers who are tired of eating junk food. You might be an atheist who suspects that there is more to Christian thought than the gurus of the New Atheism admit. More likely, you are a Christian who has been unsettled by the sneers you receive from atheist acquaintances; perhaps you are looking for something to say in reply. Is there a Christian response to Dawkins, Coyne and Myers? There certainly is: Christians have an embarrassment of academic riches to explain and defend their faith.

As a High School teacher, I have no time for intellectualism. But I can still ask for some careful thought. While I've kept this book as readable as I can, it summarises substantial arguments that the academic world takes very seriously. I ask the deepest questions a human being can ask. Why is there a universe? Who are we? Why are we here? What is wrong with the world? And I contend that a proper understanding of Christianity is essential to answering these questions.

There is no shortcut for finding answers to 'the big questions'. These questions cannot be answered by scanning a blog. We need open minds, but we also need minds that are prepared to do some *work*. We will also need stout hearts on our journey. For a strange and insidious creature stalks the internet, seeking to confound and baffle the dull witted. Take your courage in both hands, as we turn the page to face the menace that is *The Flying Spaghetti Monster*.

1

How to Slay a Spaghetti Monster

"It makes one feel such a fool."
"I know," assented the other, "but one often has to choose
between feeling a fool and being one."
GK Chesterton, The Strange Crime of John Boulnois

Mockers resent correction,
so they avoid the wise.

Sneer Pressure

I'll begin with a simple lesson for anyone who wants to teach.
You can be opinionated; you can be controversial. You can
consider the bizarre, the heretical and the reactionary. But you
can never, ever, be dogmatic. Today you might know more than
your students; one day they might know more than you. So
be patient; your students are fighting a long battle. They need
time to form their ideas, and to settle on their beliefs. And if
their opinions differ from yours, so much the better. You are
meant to free their minds from yours.

Of course, it's never pleasant to have your ideas challenged
in class. So you have several options when a student challenges

your opinions. If the student has made a simple factual error, you should correct them. If the disagreement is over interpretations, simply state why you disagree with the student. But help them to state their objection with greater clarity, and more precision. Encourage students to pursue their own ideas in their own time. The best teachers engage with opinionated students, offering guidance and even incorporating that student's viewpoints into the class.

But there is another course of action that is too tempting for many teachers to resist—especially for those in higher education. The academic holds all the cards in the lecture theatre. He *has* and he *is* the authority. So it is all too easy to ridicule the student's ideas in front of her peers. Or, at the very least, make her seem backward, ill-informed and out of fashion. Doesn't she know that her ideas have been abandoned long ago, and are dismissed in the latest publications? Who has put these ridiculous notions in her head? The student's question is not thoroughly examined. Her position is dismissed without critique. We can't have the Professor's opinions challenged by an undergraduate, can we?

This is the strategy pursued by the New Atheists. Dawkins' grasp of philosophical arguments wouldn't get him a pass grade in a high school class. But he doesn't mean to deal with the questions that theists are asking. He's ridiculing his opponents' position. The reasons for theism must be so bad, why even read about them? My goodness, no, you just dismiss them. For example, Dawkins asserts that scientists who hold orthodox Christian beliefs 'stand out for their rarity and are a subject of bafflement to their peers in the academic community.' He cites surveys to show that the majority of scientists do not believe in a personal God, and that the vast majority of Nobel Laureates are unbelievers.

In *The God Delusion* Dawkins discusses a similar tactic in a section entitled 'The Argument from Admired Religious Scientists'. There Dawkins, correctly, ridicules the idea that the existence of theistic scientists, past or present, is somehow evidence for the existence of God. So why mention that 'American scientists are less religious than the American public generally, and that the most distinguished scientists are the least religious of all' or that Nobel Laureates don't tend to be religious? If we can't use religious scientists as evidence for God's existence, why argue *against* God's existence from admired *non-religious* scientists?

So maybe Dawkins is pursuing a very different strategy. Perhaps it isn't so much that Dawkins wants young scientists reading his book to consider these statistics as evidence against the existence of God. Rather Dawkins is showing young scientists what they need to believe to fit in with the elite. No-one who wants to be considered well informed could possibly consider theism as an option. Don't they know it's all just fairy tales and imaginary friends?

We can dub this rhetorical strategy 'sneer pressure'. The aim is to gain converts by peer pressure, to make the faithful feel foolish and out of place in the modern academic environment. The reader is pressured to yield to the Professor's superior intellect, and to conform to the norms of the ideal rational community. The New Atheists have not offered one original argument for atheism. But they've plenty of original *insults*. Dawkins merely talks about theistic arguments in condescending terms, and implies that the well-educated would never take a theist seriously. If a young man or woman wishes to get ahead in the academy they should be advised to drop any religious conviction as soon as possible. This must be a sobering thought for those at the bottom of the academic food chain.

Dawn of the Spaghetti Monsters

The New Atheism aims to present theism as a backward superstition held by rednecks and suicide bombers. Theistic beliefs are not critiqued, but mocked and caricatured. And the strangest of all the caricatures is the Flying Spaghetti Monster. The monster started life as a clumsy parody of the Intelligent Design Movement. Physics graduate Bobby Henderson wrote an open letter to the Kansas State Board of Education asking if his 'Flying Spaghetti Monster' (or FSM) could have a place on the science curriculum alongside other theories of Intelligent Design.

> I and many others around the world are of the strong belief that the universe was created by a Flying Spaghetti Monster. It was He who created all that we see and all that we feel. We feel strongly that the overwhelming scientific evidence pointing towards evolutionary processes is nothing but a coincidence, put in place by Him...
>
> Some find that hard to believe, so it may be helpful to tell you a little more about our beliefs. We have evidence that a Flying Spaghetti Monster created the universe. None of us, of course, were around to see it, but we have written accounts of it. We have several lengthy volumes explaining all details of His power. Also, you may be surprised to hear that there are over 10 million of us, and growing. We tend to be very secretive, as many people claim our beliefs are not substantiated by observable evidence. [5]

The Flying Spaghetti Monster became an internet phenomenon, spawning a parody religion. It appeared on numerous websites and blogs. Bloggers began to refer to themselves as 'Pastafarians'. Someone wrote an FSM bible, someone else formulated a liturgy. Evangelistic tracts were produced. Scientific and photographic 'evidence' was fabricated to convince 'unbelievers' of the existence of the FSM. Richard Dawkins gave his blessing. All this pseudo-religious activity was manufactured in an effort to 'send up' the Christian Church. Thousands of atheists seem to think that the send-up works.

---

[5]   Bobby Henderson's full letter to the Kansas School Board can be read at: www.venganza.org/about/open-letter/ (Retrieved 16th Sept 2011).

The point of the FSM satire *seems to be* that belief in God always requires blind faith; a faith that always ignores the relevant evidence. But we can believe in *any ridiculous idea* if we have enough faith. If we ignore the evidence we can believe in whatever we choose. If it is acceptable to have blind faith in God, or the atonement, or the incarnation then we can believe in anything we like. We can have blind faith in fairies or ghosts, or Flying Spaghetti Monsters. Faith in God is deconstructed— it just looks silly in this sort of company.

This is powerful agitprop—grouping belief in God with a belief that no rational person would ever take seriously. As soon as you start to explain why belief in God is superior to belief in a piece of sentient pasta, your whole worldview sounds a bit suspect. But, as this book will show, the parody is clueless and pointless; Christianity does not depend on blind faith. The FSM parody only manages to trivialise an important debate.

How the Monster Came Out of its Teapot

The FSM is meant to update Bertrand Russell's 'celestial teapot', an argument that Richard Dawkins revived in *The God Delusion*. Richard Dawkins acknowledges that he cannot prove that God does not exist, but maintains that this is not a ground for agnosticism. Dawkins thinks that in the absence of evidence the only rational viewpoint is one of disbelief. To make his point, he draws on Bertrand Russell's story of a celestial teapot.

Suppose an astronomer claims that between Earth and Mars a teapot that it is too small to be observed, even by the most powerful telescopes, orbits the sun. Should we believe the astronomer? The teapot is so small he can't prove that it exists. But we cannot prove that it does not exist either. Since there is no evidence either way, does this mean we should be agnostic about the existence of the teapot? Should we take the view that there is a 50:50 chance that it exists?

Clearly not. In the absence of evidence, we should think that there very probably is no celestial teapot. The same, Dawkins claims, is true of God. He claims that, if there is no good evidence for the existence of God, atheism is the only rational position. He claims that when there is no evidence, we should not suspend belief. We should *disbelieve*. After all, wouldn't the onus be on adults who believe in the Tooth Fairy and Santa Claus to make their case?

Is there Life on Mars?

So the basic idea is—if there is no evidence for the existence of an entity, you should believe that the entity probably doesn't exist. That sounds like common sense on the first reading. But consider the following claims:

(a) 'Intelligent life now exists on the surface of our moon'
And
(b) 'Life exists on several planets in our universe'.

Now, we'd seem to be justified in rejecting (a). We've relatively good knowledge of our moon, and it just doesn't seem that we could find intelligent life on its surface. [6]

But we'd be much more hesitant in rejecting (b). The universe is a big place. Other 'earth-like' planets *might* be out there. But we don't know how many planets capable of sustaining life exist in our universe. We just don't have enough information to make a definitive judgment. There is a clear lesson here: in some cases, such as Santa Claus and fairies, a presumption of non-belief is appropriate. In other cases, like the possibility of plant or animal life elsewhere in our universe, it is not. What explains the difference?

Sometimes we just don't have enough *background information* to make an informed judgement. Sometimes we do. And that's the difference between believing that little green men live on the Moon and believing that a little green fungus is growing on

---

[6] See 'Probability and the Presumption of Atheism' by David Glass. A version is available at www.infj.ulst.ac.uk/~dvglass/Research/PresumptionAtheism.pdf

a planet far, far away. What we know about the Moon makes it seem unlikely that ET is attempting to make a phone call from its surface. But we do know that the universe is so vast that there's at least a chance that life exists somewhere out there. One day the human race may even find evidence of this life.

We can feel fairly confident that NASA hasn't sent crockery into orbit. So we'll dismiss the celestial teapot. So what about God? Is he like the teapot, ET on the Moon or the existence of life elsewhere in the Universe? It's a matter of considering the background information. Our knowledge of our moon *rules out* a good chance of life existing there. Our knowledge of the space exploration industry *rules out* the theory that it would waste resources by putting tea cups in space. What about Flying Spaghetti Monsters and God? Does our background knowledge mean that their existence is probable or improbable?

Nessie versus the Flying Spaghetti Monster: Whoever Wins We Lose...

Our background knowledge of the universe certainly rules out absurd entities—like living, sentient pasta with magical abilities. In our experience pasta isn't the sort of thing that goes around creating anything, never mind universes. Spaghetti doesn't typically gain mystical powers. If the FSM 'worshipper' wants to 'argue' that the FSM is made of invisible, intangible, eternal pasta, I'm afraid that I'll have to point out that we're not really talking about spaghetti anymore.

Let's take an example that is a little more tangible, just to grasp how background knowledge helps us decide which theories we should take seriously. Instead of a Spaghetti monster, let's consider the Loch Ness monster.[7] For generations, eyewitnesses

---

[7] Nessie is taken rather seriously at her home site: www.nessie.co.uk. But before you dive in, be sure to watch the excellent 1999 PBS documentary 'The Beast of Loch Ness'. A transcript of the broadcast is available www. pbs.org/wgbh/nova/transcripts/2601lochness.html

there have reported sightings of a large beast, often with at least one hump protruding from the surface waters of the loch. Some reported seeing fins or flippers on the creature. Many of these eyewitnesses were sensible, sober and well-educated.

The Loch Ness Monster ('Nessie') generated significant media interest (and several terrible movies). Scientific expeditions were organised, and in 1975 a team led by Robert Rines, a lawyer with training in physics, registered a large moving object on sonar. The team even managed to take photographs. With computer enhancement the photos revealed what appeared to be the flippers of a large aquatic animal.

Sir Peter Scott, a respected naturalist, was impressed with the photograph. This boosted the prestige of Rine's findings. But then Scott advanced a theory that caused stock in the 'Nessie' hypothesis to plummet. Scott suggested that the creature in the photograph was a Plesiosaur, a giant long-necked reptile that went extinct with the dinosaurs. This was too much for the zoological community, which dismissed Scott's idea as preposterous.

Was the zoological community right to assume that plesiosaurs do not live in the loch? In the 1970s, it would have been very difficult to prove that a beast was *not* present. Loch Ness stretches for 24 miles, and its sheer walls are 800ft deep. The loch is filled with peat particles, which limit visibility to a few feet. The steep sides play havoc with sonar, and changes in water temperature can create sonar images where no target exists. It would have been extraordinarily difficult, and prohibitively expensive, to organise an expedition to search the whole loch.

But even though zoologists could not search the loch to rule out the presence of a plesiosaur, their *background knowledge* justified their belief that plesiosaurs did not dwell in the loch. It is highly unlikely that large reptiles, like Plesiosaurs, could survive the events that eliminated the dinosaurs. If a few did somehow survive, Plesiosaurs were cold blooded creatures, and would find it difficult to live in the cold waters of Loch Ness, even if they had made their way from the ocean to the loch.

It is extremely unlikely that the loch could support a family of animals as large as Plesiosaurs. Chemical nutrients are relatively few, and the peat particles that make visibility so poor also prevent light from penetrating deep into the water. This prevents plant growth, which limits the amount of plankton that the loch can support. This leaves the loch with surprisingly few fish—certainly not enough to sustain a family of Plesiosaurs for hundreds of thousands of years.

So the background knowledge available to zoologists justified their response to Sir Peter Scott's Plesiosaur hypothesis. Background knowledge can also give us estimates on the likelihood of Vampires, Werewolves, Giant Octopi that drown bathers in North American Lakes, and strange little Mexican beasts that suckle on goat's blood. By contrast, background knowledge doesn't help us to reach a clear estimate of the probability of intelligent life existing in the visible universe. We don't know enough as yet. But in general it can give us a good idea about what is physically possible.

But how can background knowledge about the physical universe give us probabilities about things which are not physical? What about entities that exist outside space and time? In other words, does our background knowledge of the physical universe rule out the possibility that *God* exists? It can tell us a lot about many things purported to exist *in* the physical universe. But God is meant to exist *outside* the physical universe. God would be *transcendent*. God would not be made of physical parts, and he would not be limited by space, time, or the laws of nature.

Only physical beings exist in the physical universe. So it would be a circular argument to assert that the physical universe tells us that non-physical beings *can't* exist, or *probably don't* exist. Our background knowledge of the physical universe only tells us what *physical events* are probable in the *physical universe*. Knowledge of what is physically possible in our universe doesn't tell us much about what is possible *beyond* our physical universe.

How to Slay a Spaghetti Monster

So although it can teach us which *physical* beings are unlikely, it seems very unlikely that our knowledge of the physical universe can *directly* rule out transcendent, non-physical, entities. Can our background knowledge of the universe tell us nothing about how sensible it is to take the idea of God seriously? Are we doomed to agnosticism?

Not at all. We can still ask if God's existence would function as a good *hypothesis*.[8] If Theism is a good hypothesis, then we could discover that God's existence is probable. History teaches us to prefer simpler hypotheses. The fewer entities, properties, laws or kinds of entity or property postulated by a hypothesis, the simpler it is. So if theism is a simple hypothesis, it could be worth taking seriously.

That sounds a bit abstract. We can illustrate the importance of simplicity by thinking of Kepler drawing ellipses to show the path the Earth takes around the Sun. Kepler had a limited number of observations that showed the heavenly bodies at different points at different times. He could have drawn a wild, winding, circuitous path. But the ellipse was the simplest path available that accounted for the evidence. That's what he drew, and it turned out to be the best explanation.

Similarly, Newton's Theory of Motion is simple, postulating only four very general laws in its simplest formulation. Even in abstract subjects like logic and mathematics, theoreticians seek out a few simple rules that account for a potentially infinite amount of observations. And so on, and so on. The history of thought teaches us to look for simple theories.

---

[8] See Richard Swinburne's 'The Existence of God' (Oxford: 2004), especially chapters 1–6. An excellent introduction to the various analyses of a good explanation can be found in Timothy McGrew's article 'Toward a Rational Reconstruction of Design Inferences,' *Philosophia Christi* 7 (2005): 253–98.

The Simplicity of Serial Killers

Perhaps this still sounds very abstract and academic; let's illustrate our point a little more with two tragic tales. In 1912 Bessie Mundy drowned in her bath after having a seizure. In 1913 Alice Burnham was found dead in her bath in her home in Blackpool after suffering a fit and drowning. Then, in 1914, Margaret Lofty was found dead in her bath in the town of Highgate. Once more, doctors suspected that the unfortunate lady had suffered an epileptic fit.

Gradually more facts emerged which linked the three cases. All three women were recent brides. All three had made a will, with very generous terms for their husbands, just before they drowned. All three women had married exactly the same man just before they died. He had used different names on each occasion, but police soon identified George Joseph Smith as the lucrative widower. Smith never confessed to any crime, and no physical evidence tied him to the death of his wives. His defence maintained that he was unlucky in love, and hoped that judge and jury would buy that explanation.

The judge was not convinced that anyone could be *that* unlucky, and the jury opined that there was a simpler explanation available. The justice system concluded that Smith murdered each woman for money. One man motivated by greed was more likely than chance to produce these deaths; and certainly more likely than a rather unusual form of epilepsy which only occurs when the sufferer encounters warm water after writing her will. Smith was convicted of murder.

Fast forward one century. Between late October and early December 2006, five young women, all prostitutes and victims of Britain's drug culture, were murdered in the city of Ipswich. Police immediately went on the hunt for a serial killer. It was much more probable that a serial killer was responsible for all five deaths, than a vast criminal conspiracy. And even though these young women were likely to have been assaulted by clients every week, it was simpler, and more probable, that one man had escalated to murder than five different men during the same time period.[9]

Steve Wright, a dockside worker was quickly apprehended; but he maintained that he was innocent. No direct physical evidence established that Wright was involved in violent activity. (In the defence's terms, there was no 'smoking gun'.) Wright admitted to soliciting all five girls—so he had an explanation for the forensic evidence that linked him to the five victims. Finally, there was one other suspect, who had been arrested by police before Wright was charged. This suspect admitted to knowing some of the victims, and he had no alibi.

But after the first killings, the Police used Automatic Number Plate Recognition cameras to record all the vehicles frequenting Ipswich's red light district. That, and CCTV evidence, put Wright in the vicinity of each girl just before she disappeared. Wright had solicited the five girls in the exact order they had died. In fact, CCTV footage showed one of the girls getting into his car on the night that she died. Whoever disposed of the bodies had local knowledge, and Wright was a local man. He drove past the brook where two of the bodies had been found on his way to work. Forensic evidence tied him, and no-one else, to *all* the murdered girls; DNA evidence tied him to three of the girls. And blood from some of the young women had been found on his jacket.

Wright was the 'common denominator' in the disappearance and murder of all five women. By far, the simplest explanation before the jury was that Steve Wright was guilty of murder. To suggest that a series of coincidences had produced the evidence against Wright was needlessly complicated. The jury found the simplest explanation the most powerful: Steve Wright was found guilty of murder. If juries could not use the simplest

---

[9]   The tragic tales of Bessie Mundy and the Ipswich Serial Killings are both discussed with sensitivity and intelligence in Paul Harrison and David Wilson's *'Hunting Evil: Inside the Ipswich Serial Murders'*(Sphere:2008).

explanation to account for the evidence, at least one serial killer would be walking free.

Away with the Fairies

Let's do a quick stocktaking. We judge what hypotheses are worth considering by checking them against our background knowledge. We can also compare our hypothesis to theories that have turned out to be true in the past. Our best theories tend to be simple. So we want a hypothesis that is simple and coherent. And theism is certainly a simple hypothesis. One God of limitless, loving power is the foundation of everything else that exists

But is simplicity all that we need? Or should we seek for something more? Consider ghosts. These are non-physical beings (although they would have a spatial location and so, unlike God, would not transcend the physical world). Unlike the FSM, we can give ghosts a fairly simple description: disembodied agents with intentions similar to our own. So if there's no evidence against their existence, and no reason to think that they're impossible, should we remain agnostic about their existence? Can we believe in poltergeists and ghouls?

No, because there's no point in believing in a hypothesis just because it is simple. A simple and coherent hypothesis is a good place to start. But there's simply no point in believing in a hypothesis unless it explains something. A hypothesis must have *explanatory power*. Hypotheses have explanatory power if they lead us to *expect various observations; particularly observations that would be unlikely to occur if the hypothesis was false*. This is what we mean by *evidence*. [10]

Consider the Ipswich serial killer Steve Wright. Given the extensive use of police surveillance, if Wright was the killer

[10] Swinburne discusses the nature and meaning of evidence 'The Existence of God' 52–72; Elliott Sober's discussion in *Evidence and Evolution* is brief and informative (Cambridge: 2008), 1-7.

we would expect to find evidence that linked him to the murdered girls. We also would expect to find that he had some local knowledge, given where the bodies were hidden. Wright matched the criteria perfectly. On the other hand, if Wright was innocent, it would be extraordinarily unlikely to find that he solicited the five murdered girls in the order they disappeared.

'Nessie the Plesiosaur' has very little explanatory power. Yes, there have been numerous sightings of odd creatures in the loch. But we would expect to find odd sightings and sonar contacts given the murky conditions of Loch Ness. Even trained observers can mistake a log or a wake for something else. We have already mentioned that the steep sides of the loch create strange sonar contacts which could be mistaken for large moving objects. And the photographic evidence is either ambiguous (Rine's photographs) or a fake (e.g. The famous 'Surgeon's Photograph'). The 'Plesiosaur Hypothesis' is a complex theory with little or no explanatory power.

Theism claims that the universe has a *personal* cause.[11] If we believe in God we should expect to find evidence of purpose in the universe. Is there evidence of purposive activity in our universe? Does our universe contain the type of order that agents bring about? Does it have features that a rational agent would value? Absolutely! God accounts for the order that we see in our universe. God explains why the universe has conscious living knowing beings. God explains why good and evil are as real and as important as electromagnetism or gravity. God explains why humans crave purpose and meaning. We'll examine these arguments in more detail as the book progresses.

This highlights why it is wrong to compare God to invisible pixies and fairies. These examples just postulate one more entity or class of entities in the universe which don't explain

---

[11] Christians believe that God is not a single, isolated person; rather, God is three co-equal, co-eternal persons sharing the same essential nature.

anything. If theism can play an important role in explaining our universe we should take it very seriously indeed; we should not waste our time pondering crude caricatures. We might also note that meaningless and trivial stories (like the belief that invisible fairies dwell at the bottom of the garden) are so disconnected from the real world that it isn't only impossible to provide evidence *for* them. It is impossible to provide evidence *against* them. So it is very interesting that evidence can count *against* theism.

If there is a God worthy of worship, why does he allow suffering? Why is the living world so wasteful—what was the point of making those marvellous dinosaurs, just to wipe them out? Why is it not clear which religion provides the best way of approaching God? Now theists have different responses to this counter-evidence, which we'll discuss in chapter seven. But what is important to note is that it *is* counter-evidence. If it is possible to provide evidence against the existence of God, then theism is not a meaningless fairy tale.

Nothing in this chapter proves that God exists. I have only argued that theism is a simple hypothesis which could have explanatory power; and that the probability of God's existence isn't so ridiculously low that we can ignore evidence for his existence. The infantile antics of the Flying Spaghetti Monster's followers shouldn't make theists pause and reconsider their worldview. But the FSM did provide an excuse to show that the concept of God is meaningful and worthy of attention.

2

Science Falls into a Gap

> The great triumph of Humanity I had dreamed of took a
> different shape in my mind. It had been no such triumph
> of moral education and general co-operation as I had
> imagined...Its triumph had not been simply a triumph over
> Nature, but a triumph over Nature and the fellow-man.
> *HG Wells 'The Time Machine'*

> He will judge between the nations and will settle disputes
> for many peoples. They will beat their swords into
> plowshares and their spears into pruning hooks.

Claiming to be wise, they instead became utter fools

Every prophet's life follows a certain pattern. He learns that
sacred laws have been broken and that a great and terrible
judgment must follow. But the multitudes will not listen to his
warnings; only a small band of faithful witnesses are ready for
the impending apocalypse. Even in an age of declining biblical
literacy this story seems familiar, partly because Old Testament
epics survive in disaster movies. But in the disaster movie the

prophet is nearly always a scientist. The Almighty is relegated to a bit part; Science takes the place of Jehovah.

In *'Jaws'* a marine biologist cannot persuade the townsfolk of Amity that a Great White Shark is feeding on tourists; the mayor refuses to close the beaches. Dennis Quaid's paleo-climatologist in *'The Day After Tomorrow'* warns a complacent and scientifically illiterate Vice President about an impending cataclysmic climate shift. In *'Earthquake'* and *'The Towering Inferno'* Charlton Heston and Paul Newman play architects whose technical expertise is ignored by greedy construction firms, with devastating consequences.

In Science Fiction the scientist emerges not merely as a prophet, but also as a saviour. In *'Independence Day'* Jeff Golblum's MIT educated technician realises that the aliens are hostile. He then defeats the invaders by downloading a computer virus onto a flying saucer's (IBM compatible) computer. Contrast this with HG Wells' *'War of the Worlds'* in which the aliens are destroyed by bacteria—'slain, after all man's devices had failed, *by the humblest things that God, in his wisdom, has put upon this earth.*'

Where does popular culture's faith in Science come from? Brian Silver, in *The Ascent of Science*[12], notes that in 1834 the French physicist Arago was asked to explain why the French government should continue to financially support the development of the Sciences. What practical benefits had science brought the French people? Arago paused for a moment, and then offered the only example that came to his mind: the lightning conductor.

The first industrial revolution was profoundly transforming Arago's world, but science could take very little of the credit. Richard Arkwright, Samuel Crompton, James Hargreaves, and John Kay were inventors and entrepreneurs—not scientists. Perhaps Arago's comment was a little unfair to James Watt

---

[12] Brian Silver, *The Ascent of Science* (Oxford University Press, 2000). The role of Christianity in the rise of modern science is discussed in James Hannam's *'God's Philosophers: How the Medieval World Laid the Foundations of Modern Science'* (Icon:2010) and John Henry's *'The Scientific Revolution and the Origins of Modern Science'* (Palgrave MacMillan:2008), 85-97.

and Eli Whitney, but the fact remains that both men were primarily engineers and inventors—men searching for practical solutions to practical problems. Neither man studied nature in a detached manner through the method of experimentation.

But then God said 'let Faraday be', and all was taxable light. Electric power replaced steam power, and the power of the machine replaced the power of man and beast. It was science that ushered the new world of the second industrial revolution. It was probably at this stage that a new mythology became firmly rooted in popular culture. Science would uncover all mysteries, technology would build on the wisdom of science, and we would build a new heaven and a new earth.

It is easy to see why we treat science with such respect. As science progresses it not only provides *answers*; it provides *solutions* like penicillin and lasers. But the success of science causes many thinkers to get carried away. For many intellectuals the physical sciences are as good as the academy can get. In turn, this strengthens our culture's belief that science can solve every practical and social problem. It also leads many writers to assert that science can answer every existential question.

This faith in the significance of science is summed up neatly by blogger Greta Christina:

> Atheists care about science because science provides an alternate method for understanding reality...Science is a method for perceiving the world that relies, not on authority and intuition, but on rigorous examination of evidence and a willingness to question any theory. When it comes to understanding the world, science offers an alternative to religion: not merely different answers, but a different way of asking questions. Science doesn't disprove religion. It simply makes it unnecessary. Which is why it's relevant to atheism... and why atheists care about it so much.[13]

[13] Find Greta Christina's thoughts on science and atheism at www.alternet. org/story/126118/10_myths_and_truths_about_atheists_/?page=entire (retrieved 17 April 2012).

For Greta Christina science not only replaces the prophet and the saviour, science replaces religious thought altogether. This belief in the powers of science borders on blind faith. It may be true that the physical sciences have been very successful in finding out how the physical world operates. But it doesn't follow that the physical world is the only thing that exists! Important answers about meaning, purpose and morality could be missed if we restrict ourselves to the teachings of science.

New Atheists like Greta Christina, Jerry Coyne and PZ Myers seem committed to *Dogmatic Scientism*. They argue that we should only believe what the physical sciences teach us; that the physical sciences will eventually provide answers to every question worth asking, and provide the only hope for human flourishing and progress. Now *Dogmatic Scientism* is a big claim. It's attempting to tell us how to reason about life, the universe and everything. Scientific theories usually avoid claims of this scope. So *Dogmatic Scientism* doesn't seem very scientific. It seems more akin to philosophy or theology.

Worse, *Dogmatic Scientism* does not follow from any scientific theory. It is not the result of any scientific experiment. And there is no reason to suppose that *Dogmatic Scientism* will be included in the completed physical sciences (what science will tell us when scientists have answered every scientific question.) In fact, the turbulent and sometimes revolutionary history of science should make us hesitate before we predict what the completed physical sciences will look like.

In other words, if you believe *Dogmatic Scientism* you have a problem. You're telling others that they should only believe what science teaches. But science doesn't teach *Dogmatic Scientism* in any of its theories or experimental results! So, others shouldn't believe *Dogmatic Scientism,* and neither should you. Opposition to *Dogmatic Scientism* logically cannot be identical with opposition to science in general. This shouldn't come as a surprise. After all, literature, history and philosophy teach us that scientific explanations are not the only explanations in town.

Calling All Agents...

Scientific explanations deal with impersonal objects and laws of nature; we observe and measure how some events regularly follow others. We then use our knowledge of these regularities to explain some state of affairs. For example, we can explain why Mars is in its present location by describing the solar system, where the planets have been recently and Newton's laws of gravity. Or, scientific explanations can explain objects by breaking them down into their constituent parts to understand how they form structures. So we can see how atoms form molecules, and how molecules can form cells.

But there is more to our world than the impersonal; we cannot understand or predict human activity without talking about *persons* and *purposes*. We don't need scientific knowledge of another person's brain states to explain their actions. We need only think of ourselves, and others, as *persons* (or *agents*) who *have purposes and can act on them*[14]. These concepts are coherent, clear, and plausible and they generate good and useful predictions. It's very difficult to know what else we should ask from an explanation.

Some thinkers would insist that we are wrong to treat humans as agents. They argue that every human is a product of his genetic nature, of his environment, and of his life experience. We do not choose how our brain and nervous systems react in different situations. Like everything else in the universe, we're just caught up in a chain of cause and effect. On this view of humans, we do not control our actions; events just *happen* to us. We are not *agents*; our nervous systems just act and react.

But without a belief in *agency* we cannot hold people accountable for their actions. If an aeroplane crashes because

[14] Discussions of 'Agent Explanation' can be found in EJ Lowe '*A Survey of Metaphysics*' (New York: Oxford University Press: 2002), 195-213; Richard Swinburne '*The Existence of God*' (Oxford: 2008) 35-45; and Paul K Moser '*The Evidence for God*'(Cambridge: 2010), 48-63

it lost a wing, we don't blame the aeroplane. There's a clear scientific explanation that appeals to *events, and only events*. Once that wing goes, the law of gravity takes over. One event causes another, and the aeroplane inevitably falls to the ground. However, we might blame the plane's manufacturer if he used inferior material to maximise profits. He formed a purpose and acted on it.

We can illustrate the difference between a *scientific* explanation that appeals to *events* and a *personal* explanation that appeals to *agency* by considering the children's film *'The Iron Giant'*. Set at the height of the Cold War, Brad Bird's award winning film re-imagines the children's novel by poet Ted Hughes. A young boy, Hogarth, discovers a giant robot near his home on the coast of Maine. The audience gradually becomes aware that this machine has been sent to attack our planet; however, when it crash-landed it sustained serious damage to its skull. This seems to have wiped its programming, transforming it into a rather placid and friendly behemoth.

The giant becomes Hogarth's playmate, and Hogarth tries to hide it from the paranoid government official investigating reports of a UFO landing. But, inevitably, the US military catches up with Giant, and attempts to destroy it. In the battle, Hogarth is knocked unconscious. The giant assumes that his friend is dead; his anger triggers his original programming and he attacks the military with lethal force. The giant activates numerous advanced weapons systems, and destroys the armed forces surrounding it. In the panic, an officer calls in a nuclear strike that will not only destroy the robot, but Hogarth's home town as well.

Up to this point of the film the Iron Giant had been at the mercy of his computer and his programming. While it was damaged, the Giant acted placidly. When its programming was restored, the Giant simply followed the path its makers mapped out for it. The Giant was controlled by *events* in its mechanical brain. These events caused desires and beliefs; and these beliefs and desires caused the giant to act in certain ways. The Giant was nothing more than an automaton.

But then Hogarth revives, catches up to his friend, and treats him like an *agent*. He tells him the town is doomed without the Giant's help; but the Giant does not have to be a killer. 'You are who you choose to be!' The giant is reminded of his friendship with the young boy. And now, with all his conflicting beliefs and desires, the robot must make a *choice*. Persuaded of the value of human life, and his own desire to be like the heroes in Hogarth's comic books, The Iron Giant chooses to sacrifice himself and save his friend. He flies directly into the oncoming missile, and is (seemingly) destroyed by the nuclear blast.

The movie's ending is a cliché; but that only goes to show how familiar agent explanations are. We all sympathize with the movie's premise that there is more to the Giant than the events in its head; we all know how it feels to choose between conflicting desires. When he is attacking the soldiers, the Giant is at the mercy of his programming. *Events* in the Giant's mechanical brain explain his violence. However, when he *chooses* to plot a crash course with the oncoming nuclear missile, the events in the Giant's brain are at the mercy of his *purposes*. The Giant is acting as *an agent*, not a machine. We cannot understand his actions without knowing *who* he is and *the purpose* of his sacrifice.

God-of-the-Gaps: A Guide for the Perplexed

We have established that there are two types of explanation that we can use to make sense of the world. There are scientific explanations, which explain events by appealing to impersonal laws and objects; and there are agent explanations, which appeal to the purposes and abilities of persons. Now, we have a concept of one agent, God, who has the power to explain the order, structure and complexity of our universe.

But, even if a personal explanation that appeals to God is a theoretical possibility, Richard Dawkins insists we simply have no need of it: 'Historically, religion aspired to explain our own existence and the nature of the universe in which we find ourselves. In this role it is now completely superseded by science.' Dawkins is raising the spectre of the 'God of the Gaps'. People once appealed to the gods to explain natural events beyond their ken. However, as it uncovered the mechanisms that govern nature, science *explained God away*. We no longer appeal to Thor or Baal to explain lightning, because we understand the nature of electricity.

To understand the nature of 'explaining away', consider the death of Princess Diana by a car accident in an underpass by the River Seine. Such tragedies define a generation, and many believe that such events do not occur at random. Conspiracy theorists discern sinister forces at work. Diana was the mother of the heir to the British throne, and her boyfriend, Dodi al-Fayed, was a Muslim. The forces of British conservatism were horrified by their courtship. So wasn't it something of a coincidence that both Diana *and* Dodi perished in the same crash? Isn't it probable that British Intelligence engineered the 'accident' to rid the Queen of a troublesome Princess?

This conspiracy required numerous agents with fiendishly complicated plans. Spies followed Dodi and Diana for months, waiting their opportunity. When a chance presented itself one agent spiked their chauffeur's drink. Then another followed them by car, so that he could blind that driver with a dazzling light. The British Secret Service then persuaded French authorities to arrange a cover-up. The conspirators' exact motives are still a little unclear. Diana had previously dated a Muslim doctor without controversy; marriage to a Muslim would have caused no constitutional crisis. In any case there is no compelling evidence that Dodi and Diana were engaged or contemplating marriage.

Such conspiracy theories are extraordinarily complex. They hypothesise numerous agents with vast resources, subtle motives and convoluted schemes. They can account for every piece of evidence, but the price is an ever increasing complexity as more and more layers are added to the conspiracy to explain away the counter-evidence. The conspiracy theory can account for Diana's death; but it is so complex that it hardly seems rational to consider it at all. Which leads us back to the lesson of the last chapter; if a complex theory can be avoided it should be.

In fact there is a much simpler explanation: this was a tragic accident. Dodi's chauffeur, Henri Paul, lost control of the car because he had consumed a considerable amount of alcohol, and was driving well over the legal limit. Paul was speeding to avoid crowds of paparazzi. Unfortunately neither Diana nor Dodi were wearing a seat belt. The simplest and neatest explanation of all the facts is that Henri Paul drove dangerously whilst attempting to protect Dodi and Diana from the attention of the pursuing photographers. And that is what the official French inquiry, and Lord John Stevens official British investigation, concluded.[15]

In this case the hypothesis of an accident '*explains away*' the need for a conspiracy theory. The accident 'hypothesis' explains all the evidence, and removes any need for a conspiracy theory. We can account for all the facts without a network of villainous Lords and Dukes orchestrating the entire affair with the help of MI6. Now Dawkins, and New Atheists in general, believe that science similarly 'explains away' any evidence for the existence of God. Isaac Newton once argued that God guaranteed the predictable orbits of the planets. LaPlace showed that we had no need of that hypothesis. William Paley believed that God designed the body plans of complex organisms. Charles Darwin argued that Natural Selection could do that job without any divine tinkering.

Little by little, science is explaining God away—or so the

[15] Lady Diana died August 31st, 1997. A full discussion of the conspiracy theories inspired by her death can be found in David Aaronovitch *Voodoo Histories* (Vintage:2010), 141–161.

story goes. But if we pause for a moment's reflection, we can see that science is doing no such thing. One explanation can explain another away only when the two explanations are *incompatible*. Lord Stephen's finding of an accident explains a conspiracy theory away because Diana's death cannot have been *both* a tragic accident *and* murder. But we can gain a deeper understanding of Diana's death by moving beyond the immediate causes of the accident. We cannot understand Diana's death, and its impact, without understanding the destructive power of the free press in contemporary society.

Diana was travelling at high speeds to escape the attention of a horde of free-lance photographers. Why were the photographers so keen to photograph Diana? Why was Diana so desperate to escape the paparazzi that she would allow her chauffeur to drive recklessly? While the media did not intentionally hound Diana to her death, their pursuit of the Princess was relentless, ruthless and deadly. The destructive power of the media plays an important role in explaining Diana's death. It does not conflict with the finding of an accident. In fact, it helps explain why an accident took place.

In the same way, theism illuminates the success of science. It is true that, over centuries, scientists have discovered laws of nature, and physical processes, which explain many of our observations. But, as Kepler, Galileo and Bacon would have told us, these discoveries do not explain God away. The first scientists were motivated to search for laws and mechanisms in nature *precisely because* they believed the universe was designed by a rational agent; they *expected* to find an ordered rational structure in nature. Theism and science are compatible because theism encourages us to seek laws and mechanisms out. Theistic explanations and scientific explanations are not in conflict.

Explaining the Bloodlands

Let's reflect a little more on the nature of explaining away.

Ian Kershaw follows most historians when he argues that 'without Hitler, and the unique regime he headed, the creation of a programme to bring about the physical elimination of the Jews of Europe would have been unthinkable'. Yet in *'Bloodlands: Europe Between Hitler and Stalin'*[16] Timothy Snyder draws attention to Heinrich Himmler's role. Himmler was not only the head of the SS; Hitler had also charged Himmler with 'strengthening Germandom.' Essentially, Himmler was to establish the racial superiority of the German people. Still, Himmler was locked in a contest with several other leading Nazis for Hitler's favour and political clout.

Then Germany invaded the USSR. This was a tremendous opportunity for Himmler. He could extend his racial policies into the Soviet Union as the German Army conquered territory. He ordered the slaughter of Jews, eventually insisting that women and children be shot alongside Jewish men. He directed the murders, controlled the bureaucracy and inspected the results. The result was homicide on an industrial scale. Himmler believed that he was creating a racial paradise for the German people; but he was also accruing more and more manpower, and gaining more political clout in the Nazi regime.

In September 1941, Hitler decided to expel German Jews into Eastern Europe. The ghettoes in Poland were already overcrowded. Some Nazi governors decided that it was easier to murder Jewish refugees than to house them; but it was Himmler who sought, and found, the most effective means of extermination. It was Himmler's clients who founded Belzec. This was not a 'concentration camp' where inmates would be worked to death. Death camps like Belzec existed solely to poison men, women and children by the thousand. Trains transported millions of innocents to the gas chambers, where they would die within a few hours of arrival.

[16] Timothy Snyder's *Bloodlands: Europe Between Hitler and Stalin* (Vintage:2011) and Ian Kershaw's *Hitler* (Penguin:2008) are harrowing but enlightening.

So does Himmler's opportunism *explain away* Hitler's responsibility for the Holocaust? Not at all—and Snyder and other historians are clear on this point. Himmler could only succeed insofar as he pleased Hitler; therefore Himmler's actions actually *confirm* Hitler's responsibility for the Holocaust. Himmler understood the Fuhrer's utopian ambitions better than most; indeed he shared them. And he also knew that the key to greater power was always to anticipate and then meet Hitler's expectations.

By late 1941 the German advance into Russia had stalled. At the same time America joined the war against Nazism. Hitler's dream of building a vast German empire in the East was slipping away from him. So Hitler rewrote the script; the war was no longer a war for German empire. It was a war against Jewry—the eternal enemy of the German people. 'The world war is here' he told his most trusted henchmen 'and the annihilation of Jewry must be the necessary consequence'. This was the Reich's last achievable goal, and the Nazis devoted precious resources to the elimination of over 6 million people.

The decision to expel Jews from Germany in 1941, Germany's failure to conquer Russia, and the ambitions of Heinrich Himmler all go some way to explaining the Holocaust. But they do not 'explain away' Hitler's responsibility. The evil of the Holocaust would not have occurred without Hitler's warped racial ideology and his pathological hatred of the Jewish people. Historians will continue to find other factors that made the Holocaust possible; but Hitler's political vision must remain central to any explanation of the Holocaust. Himmler's actions do not explain away the Fuhrer's guilt; *they confirm it.*

Why God Won't Be Explained Away

Scientific explanations do not explain theism away, because they *confirm* the hypothesis that our Universe has been designed. Explanations for the motion of the planets, or mechanisms like photosynthesis, do not 'explain God away'. The revelations of science raise *further questions*—questions that point to a theistic answer. Why do we live in a universe that is governed by laws and mechanisms? Why did the history of life on earth result in such bewildering diversity and beautiful complexity? Theism answers that the universe was created, and is ordered, by a rational agent—God.

Jerry Coyne was not impressed when biologist Kenneth Miller argued that: 'the fact that there are "laws" (regularities, really) in the Universe can be understood only as an act of God...' Coyne sneered that this was just another 'God-of-the Gaps' argument.

> The last claim is in fact a God-of-the-gaps argument, since it asserts that the best answer to the question, 'Why are there scientific laws at all?' is 'God made them.' Here Miller merely swaps ignorance for 'God' ...[17]

Miller's argument is that theism explains why our universe contains an incomprehensible number of particles which all follow ordered patterns; an order which is so exquisite it can be described in the simple mathematical equations. Our universe did not have to be like this. We can conceive of universes in which particles are not governed by laws but rather act randomly. There are innumerably more ways for a universe to be disordered than there are for a universe to be ordered.

So why does our universe have such remarkable order and structure? It cannot be sheer dumb luck. Surely, it isn't wildly implausible to suggest that a creator has ordered our universe this way? However, to Coyne's mind, Miller was pointing to something Science was not yet able to explain, and assuming that this provided evidence for God's existence. 'God' is just what we say when we can't explain something. Science will inevitably come up with a more satisfying explanation in time.

[17] Jerry Coyne's response to Kenneth Miller can be read at whyevolutionistrue. wordpress.com/2009/06/16/science-vs-theism-a-debate-with-kenneth-miller-part-i-throat-clearing/ (retrieved 1st July 2010).

But Coyne's objection is confused. Miller was not pointing to *gaps* in our scientific accounts of nature, but to facts that science cannot explain *in principle*. Scientific explanations appeal to impersonal laws and objects. Now some laws (Kepler's) can be explained by other laws (Newton's); these, in turn, might be explained by further laws (Einstein's). But sooner or later we'll reach a set of laws that are just foundational. They won't be explained by any other law. At this point scientific explanation breaks down. Science can't explain why there are laws of nature *because it needs the laws of nature to give explanations.*

Physics cannot explain why there are laws of physics; so there are no 'gaps' in the scientific account that can be filled by later discoveries. God, however, provides a simple and powerful *agent explanation* for the laws of nature. God would have the power to make the universe behave in a law-like manner, and the beauty and order of our cosmos is something a rational agent would value. And we know that rational agents bring about ordered states of affairs, through art, law, poetry, music, and games.

Perhaps New Atheists would object that theistic explanations are pseudo-explanations because they do not propose a physical force, or physical mechanism, that we can observe and measure. But this objection would beg the question. *Theistic explanations contend that the universe cannot be given an adequate explanation in terms of physical forces and mechanisms.* Theistic explanations are *agent explanations;* and agent explanations argue that there is more to the world than physical forces and mechanisms!

The Moral Gap

So science cannot explain God away because, as the first scientists insisted, there is no incompatibility between theism and science. From the perspective of Christian theism, science is a great good that enables us to understand the wisdom of our creator. Furthermore, while the laws of nature cannot be ultimately explained by science, theism explains why the Universe behaves in an orderly fashion. Not only is science unable to explain theism away; the laws of nature confirm the truth of theism.

Science and theism are not in direct competition; scientific theories explain different events and objects *within* the universe. *Theism explains the universe as a whole, not just the different parts and events within it.* Providing evidence for God wouldn't be like providing evidence for a type of particle or the Loch Ness Monster. We're not (merely) talking about the existence of one more entity, or type of entity, *in* the universe. Rather, we are trying to explain the nature of the *entire* universe; and theists argue that it makes sense to interpret the universe *as a creation.*

So the *scope* of the data that theism tries to explain is just too large to compare theism to a scientific theory. If God is real, we must change our view of the whole nature of the whole universe. The significance of *every part* of the cosmos changes if God created it. We would no longer view creation as the result of purposeless impersonal laws causing meaningless events. Rather the universe, in every part, would have an *agent* explanation. So if the universe has the appearance of purpose and design it provides evidence for a rational creator.

In fact, the findings of science provoke further questions that require God as an answer. But surely science provides the best prospect for human progress? Isn't technological advance mankind's only hope, given crises like global warming and the population explosion? That is doubtful. Scientific progress could face severe practical obstacles. Science cannot rewrite human nature. While it might enhance human capabilities one day, humans will still act in whatever way seems best to them.

Humans act irrationally; our best ideas are often repressed or excised in the war of all against all. Furthermore our laws and institutions, our customs and cultures, are all inherently fragile and susceptible to violence. We live in a society which nurtures specific values and skills, and provides the economic resources, which enable large scale in-depth scientific research. If that social structure should fall, scientific progress will fall with it. Without communities that value wisdom and truth, the pursuit of science will falter and die.

So consider the paradox that pop culture's faith in science cannot resolve. The very power that scientific progress has brought to society makes that society vulnerable. We can now devour resources and destroy life at unprecedented rates. Simply reflect on the power that scientific progress put in the hands of a Soviet nuclear submarine commander during the Cuban missile crisis. If we ignore the anarchy that reigns in the human heart, the very power of scientific discovery could bring scientific progress to a terrible end.

3

Design, Dawkins,
and the Problem with Having a Big Brain

'Any intelligent fool can make things more complex; but it
takes a touch of genius to move in the opposite direction.'
Albert Einstein

Hear, O Israel, the Lord your God is one!

PZ Myers, New Atheist *extraordinaire*, responds to the learned
criticisms of Richard Dawkins' 'The God Delusion' with
a parable: 'the Courtier's Reply.'[18] This story describes an
episode which took place after the events of 'the Emperor's
New Clothes'. The Emperor in PZ Myer's sequel represents the
Church and the non-existent 'clothes' worn by the Emperor
are religious beliefs. The young boy, who has pointed out that
the Emperor is not wearing any clothes, symbolises Richard
Dawkins. Richard has just embarrassed the Emperor by

---

[18] Myers' infamous 'parable' can be read at scienceblogs.com/
pharyngula/2006/12/the_courtiers_reply.php (retrieved 30th Dec 2011).

pointing out that his majesty is naked. The Emperor's subjects can now enjoy a hearty chuckle at their ridiculous ruler.

In Myer's parable the Emperor decides to strike back. He commissions the court intellectuals to pen a letter which explains why the little boy was in error. In contrast to the youngster, many of society's intellectuals *adored* the Emperor's new clothes. The letter reads thus:

> I have considered the impudent accusations of Mr Dawkins with exasperation at his lack of serious scholarship. He has apparently not read the detailed discourses of Count Roderigo of Seville on the exquisite and exotic leathers of the Emperor's boots, nor does he give a moment's consideration to Bellini's masterwork, *On the Luminescence of the Emperor's Feathered Hat*. We have entire schools dedicated to writing learned treatises on the beauty of the Emperor's raiment, and every major newspaper runs a section dedicated to imperial fashion; Dawkins cavalierly dismisses them all. He even laughs at the highly popular and most persuasive arguments of his fellow countryman, Lord D. T. Mawkscribbler, who famously pointed out that the Emperor would not wear common cotton, nor uncomfortable polyester, but must, I say must, wear undergarments of the finest silk.
>
> Dawkins arrogantly ignores all these deep philosophical ponderings to crudely accuse the Emperor of nudity.
>
> Personally, I suspect that perhaps the Emperor might not be fully clothed—how else to explain the apparent sloth of the staff at the palace laundry—but, well, everyone else does seem to go on about his clothes, and this Dawkins fellow is such a rude upstart who lacks the wit of my elegant circumlocutions, that, while unable to deal with the substance of his accusations, I should at least chide him for his very bad form.
>
> Until Dawkins has trained in the shops of Paris and Milan, until he has learned to tell the difference between a ruffled flounce and a puffy pantaloon, we should all pretend he has not spoken out against the Emperor's

taste. His training in biology may give him the ability to recognize dangling genitalia when he sees it, but it has not taught him the proper appreciation of Imaginary Fabrics.

Myer's argument can be summarised thus:

1) Theistic belief is analogous to the Emperor's belief that he was wearing new clothes—that is to say, theism is obviously false, absurd and dangerous.

2) Of course theists have arguments that attempt to show that Theism is not obviously false, absurd and dangerous.

3) But we don't need to consider those arguments as theism is obviously false, absurd and dangerous.

New Atheists are reduced to such circular arguments because they are selling a feeling; the assurance that unbelief is infinitely superior to theistic superstition. If a New Atheist acknowledged that there was a smidgen of evidence for God's existence, then theism would cease to be a superstition. The atheist's sense of superiority would suddenly seem unwarranted. So writers like Myers make a virtue of their ignorance. They do not expand their minds by considering the alternatives to atheism; they do not research their opponents. New Atheists don't study up; they dumb up.

Dealing with Design

So which arguments should PZ Myers consider? Many theists argue that the exquisite order of our universe is compelling evidence for the existence of God. But New Atheists feel that they have an unanswerable reply to the design argument. The evidence for a designer can be explained away by the theory of evolution. Greta Christina summarises:[19]

---

[19] Greta Christina's attack on the design argument can be found gretachristina.typepad.com/greta_christinas_weblog/2010/05/argument-from-design.html (retrieved 19th Nov 2012).

> The argument from design argues that the evidence for God lies in the seemingly inexplicable complexity and functionality and balance of life: of individual life forms, of specific biological organs and systems, of the ecosystem itself. 'Look at the eye!' the argument goes. 'Look at an ant colony! Look at a bat's sonar! Look at symbiotic relationships between species! Look at the human brain! They work so well! They do such astonishing things! Are you trying to tell me that these things just... happened? How can you possibly explain all that without a designer?'

Not to be snarky, but: Have you heard of this Darwin fellow?

Just to reassure Greta that I have heard of Darwin, and some of the science based on his work, I'll give a brief description of the theory of evolution. All living things descended from one form of life, which arose some four billion years ago. Offspring inherit traits from their parents with a high degree of reliability. However, traits are not reproduced with perfect reliability. There is some variation and some creatures are born with traits that they did not inherit. There are insufficient resources for every organism to survive and reproduce; some organisms have traits that give them an advantage in the reproductive stakes. Through this process of natural selection, organisms become better and better adapted to their environments, acquiring distinctive features and novel forms.[20]

Evolution by natural selection does more than give an unified account of the history of life on earth, or tell us how new species form. For Richard Dawkins the central problem of evolutionary biology is the existence of complex adaptation. How could intricately complicated adaptations like the vertebrate eye exist unless they were designed? It is inconceivable that a fully formed eye could form by accident: it simply has

---

[20] For a survey of different conceptions of evolution read Kim Sterelny, '*Dawkins v Gould: Survival of the Fittest*' (Icon: 2007). For a discussion of the role of chance in evolution see Elliott Sober's '*Evidence and Evolution*' (Cambridge:2008).

too many parts which must be arranged in the correct way. But Darwin showed that design and purely random 'all-at-once' events were not the only options. The evolution of the eye, for example, did not occur all at once. It happened gradually, over thousands of generations.

A simple light-sensitive spot on the skin of some ancestral creature gave it an advantage by allowing it to detect and move towards light sources, thereby aiding photosynthesis. It passed this advantage to its descendants. Then, in one descendant, random changes created a depression in the light-sensitive patch, effectively placing it in a little 'cup', which enabled that creature to better detect the direction of the light. More random changes in one of its descendants would cause little 'pin holes' to develop over the cup, greatly increasing resolution and imaging. More and more specialised cells would evolve over time until we have the camera type eyes characteristic of vertebrates.

Mathematical modelling indicates that the octopus eye could have evolved in 2000 steps occurring over 400 000 generations. The process need not have taken more than 500 000 years. Only a little 'luck' was needed at each stage of the eye's development, and each 'improvement' of the eye was preserved by natural selection. The mechanisms involved were normal physical and chemical processes. There was no need for a divine engineer to tinker with cells. Biology need only appeal to physical events, making it as 'scientific' as Physics or Chemistry.

Would biology become any more 'atheistic' than Chemistry or Physics if evolution can account for organised complexity? In the preface to *Should Christians Embrace Evolution?* conservative evangelical theologian Wayne Grudem states:[21]

> ...when atheists assure us that *matter + evolution + 0 = all living things*, and then theistic evolutionists answer, no, that *matter + evolution + God = all living things*, it will not take long for unbelievers to conclude that, therefore, *God = 0*.

[21] Read his thoughts online shouldchristiansembraceevolution.com/foreword.

Perhaps many unbelievers do reason this way; if so, their reasoning is deeply flawed. No one can claim that matter + evolution + 0 = all living things. The most that anyone can claim is that a very specific kind of matter + very specific laws + very specific initial conditions of our universe = life is possible. The atheist still needs to explain why we live in the right type of universe with the right physical laws. Particles must have very specific properties, and be able to combine in very specific ways, to form elements like carbon, hydrogen and oxygen. If those atoms could not be arranged in particular patterns the organic compounds essential for life could not occur.

One's opinion of Intelligent Design or Creationism is beside the point (although both are dismissed too casually by the intelligentsia). Evolution is a poor excuse for atheism. *Even if* Coyne and Dawkins are correct, *even if* 'evolution is true', *evolution could not occur without very specific conditions*! If the force of gravity was even slightly weaker every star would be a red dwarf; if it was slightly stronger, every star would be a blue giant. In either case, life would not be possible. Several other basic physical constants must be 'fine-tuned' for a universe of galaxies, stars, planets and biological life.

The cosmological constant, the strong and electromagnetic forces, gravity, the weak force, the proton/neutron difference, and carbon production in stars all needed to have values that fell within a very narrow range. The probability of all being 'fine-tuned' to life-permitting values turns out to be less than 1 in 10^{100}. To give you a sense of the size of that number, there are only 10^{80} subatomic particles in the known universe! The universe gives every indication of being 'set up' for life.[22]

Furthermore, to *explain away* the evidence for design, natural selection needs to do much more than account for complex adaptations, like the eye or the ear. It also needs to explain why life managed to make all the transitions from bacteria and algae to birds, reptiles and mammals. Granted, most evolutionary

---

[22]   Alvin Plantinga, *Where the Conflict Really Lies* (Oxford: 2012), 198.

biologists would expect some increase in complexity over time. But the journey from the first cells to human beings requires numerous transitions, some less probable than others. It is this journey that stands in need of explanation.

Imagine all the evolutionary transitions that would need to take place to get from the first cells all the way up to us. As Elliott Sober has pointed out:

> Even if each transition in this chain—from the first to the second, from the second to the third, and so on—were highly probable, it would not follow that the transition from the first to the last is highly probable. The problem is that probabilities multiply; multiply a big probability like 9999/10000 by itself enough times and you obtain a probability that is very small indeed.[23]

And in *The God Delusion* Richard Dawkins concedes that some key transitions in life's history were incredibly *improbable*. Dawkins believes that the origin of the first cells was statistically improbable. It was also extremely unlikely that life would evolve past the level of bacteria, and even more unlikely that the complex nervous systems necessary for consciousness would evolve. Dawkins testimony is that evolution, unaided, does *not* fully explain why *human* life exists on *Earth*.

Dawkins argues instead that evolution explains why human life exists *in a universe which contains billions of Earth-like planets*. While intelligent life failed to evolve on the vast majority of these planets, on our planet the cards fell just right. There are billions of planets that have developed life at the level of bacteria, but only a fraction of these life forms ever made it across the gap to

---

[23] Sober's comments on dwindling probabilities are from his review of Simon Conway Morris's '*Life's Solution*' philosophy.wisc.edu/sober/morris%20 review%20for%20NYT.pdf. Sober is not a theist, and is one of the design argument's most articulate and penetrating critics.

something like the eukaryotic cell. And of these, a yet smaller fraction managed to cross the later Rubicon to consciousness.[24]

And what is Dawkins' evidence for these billions of life-bearing planets? He doesn't present any! To 'explain away' the evidence of design, Dawkins would need to calculate the probability of intelligent life evolving on Earth. Suppose he came up with an answer of a trillion to one. Then he would need to show that evolution has taken place on something close to a trillion planets. These planets require the right type of solar system, the right atmosphere, the right geology and many other conditions. There could be fewer planets capable of supporting higher mammals than Star Trek fans would like to believe. Dawkins hypothesises that chance, plus evolution, plus billions of opportunities on Earth-like planets explains appearance of design in the living world. That hypothesis leads to a prediction: even if we found trillions of Earth-like planets, the majority would be lifeless, a small fraction would have bacterial life, and we would only find conscious animals on the tiniest fraction. However, suppose we discovered that all of these planets were teeming with creatures like birds and mammals. Dawkins' hypothesis would be falsified.

The point is that Dawkins is helping himself to billions of worlds, then telling us what life is like on those worlds; and he is doing this without a shred of evidence. To put it as gently as possible, that doesn't seem like much of an objection to the design argument. It can't explain the laws of nature or 'fine-tuning' nor does it explain away the wonders of the living world around us.

---

[24] Dawkins argues that 'sheer luck' bridges major gaps in the evolutionary story in *The God Delusion* 168–9. 'Our planet must be one of the intensely rare planets that has bridged all three gaps.' (He means the origin of life, the origin of eukaryotic cells and the origin of consciousness.) But the universe might not have the 'billions and billions' of life-supporting planets that Dawkins requires. See John Gribbin *'The Reason Why: The Miracle of Life on Earth'* (Allen Lane:2011).

Richard Dawkins: Darwin's Rottweiler? Or Hume's Poodle?

Yet, Dawkins insists that theism has no explanatory power because theism is as complex as a hypothesis gets. His reasoning is remarkably straightforward. Theists often use God to explain highly improbable events, like the origin of complex living cells. Cells have numerous parts that must be arranged in a precise manner for the cell to function. It is extremely improbable that a cell would arise merely by chance. So the *organised complexity* of the cell demands an explanation.

But Dawkins insists that God cannot explain organised complexity because a designer's mind would also be organised and complex. After all, the only system known to be capable of design is the human brain. The brain has much more organised complexity than a living cell. Naturally, we seek explanations for the existence of the brain. But God's mind has much more organised complexity than the human brain! If the organised complexity in a cell or brain stands in need of explanation, how much more the organised complexity of God's mind? Saying that God designed the universe just leads to the question 'Well, who designed the designer'? At first glance, this seems like a powerful objection to the simplicity of theism.

To some extent we can attribute this argument to the 18th Century philosopher David Hume. Hume argued that *no* design argument could *ever* succeed.

> We are still obliged to mount higher in order to find the cause of this cause which you had assigned as satisfactory and conclusive. ... a mental world or universe of ideas requires a cause as much as does a material world or universe of objects, and, if similar in its arrangement, must require a similar cause.[25]

Hume's language is a little antiquated, but he is essentially making the same argument as Dawkins in *The God Delusion*.

---

[25] The quotation of Hume is taken from *'Dialogues Concerning Natural Religion'*.

Basically, Hume is saying that God's mind would contain so many ideas that it would be more complex than the universe it is supposed to explain. This leads us to ask, 'Who designed God's mind?' Hume seemed to believe that minds were just collections of ideas; but Hume's metaphysics seem a little odd in the modern scientific age. So Dawkins is, quite deliberately, popularising and updating Hume's argument.

A crucial point follows. Science does not overturn the design argument. As Darwin's agnostic ally, Thomas Huxley, pointed out 'the doctrine of evolution does not even come into contact with Theism, considered as a philosophical doctrine.'[26] Even if we accept the modern scientific consensus, and agree that evolution by natural selection adequately explains the history of life on earth, we are left with a further question: *Why is evolution possible?* Dawkins knows that we need to explain why the laws of physics and chemistry, and extraordinarily precise cosmological constants, allowed evolution to occur in the first place.

Furthermore, why did evolution take a course that resulted in a beautifully complex world and rational beings? This outcome was extremely improbable! The theory of evolution does not rid the world of a designer. So Dawkins is forced to use David Hume's *philosophical* argument—that God lacks an explanation because God would be more complex than the world he created. But Dawkins' impatience with philosophy of religion is notorious, and he makes no attempt to understand the worldview he is critiquing. This leaves Dawkins confined to the limits of his own speculation. He makes what we can call a 'Big Brain' Assumption. He assumes that God would be like a very big, indescribably complex brain.

> God may not have a brain made of neurones, or a CPU made of silicon, but if he has the powers attributed to him he must have something far more elaborately and non-randomly constructed than the largest brain or the largest

[26] The full Huxley quotation can be read in context at aleph0.clarku.edu/huxley/CE2/GeNan.html

computer we know.

Here Dawkins makes a humiliating blunder. He assumes that God must be made of something. Now that's an astonishing error. *By definition God would not be made of anything.* God is defined as *the creator.* That's what the term 'God' means! *By hypothesis* God cannot be an arrangement of parts. If God were made of parts then those parts would be more fundamental than God, and God would not be the creator. So once you start asking what God is made of you just sound silly. You clearly have not understood the hypothesis that you are criticising.

Why on earth should we think that God is like a computer or a brain in any sense at all? Dawkins' doesn't say. Perhaps Dawkins could argue that every intelligent being we have ever encountered has a brain. Brains presumably have the moving parts, internal linkages, and changing states required for computation. So if God is intelligent he must have the 'spiritual equivalent' of moving parts, internal linkages, and changing states.

This would be what philosophers call a weak inductive argument—all observed As have been B, so all As are probably B. Every intelligent being that we have encountered has a complex brain. Therefore, God is likely to have a complex brain. Every swan I have encountered is white. Therefore, I will never encounter a black swan. Our economic policy has not failed us in the past; therefore it will not fail us in the future. When used carelessly, simple inductive generalisations easily lead us into silly and dangerous errors.

In any case, the constant conjunction of terrestrial intelligence and brains would not establish that God would be like a 'Big Brain'. At the very most, it only follows that every 'physical intelligence' (or 'embodied intelligence') has parts, links and changing states. However, we established in the first chapter that God would exist *outside* the physical universe. God would be *transcendent.* He could not be made of physical parts, and he would not be limited by space, time, or the laws of nature. This would mean that God is rather unlike anything that we have directly experienced on earth.

If we limit our ideas of what is possible to what we have experienced, we can make dangerous errors. Furthermore, physics teaches us not to limit our beliefs to what we have experienced, *or even to what we can picture in our imaginations.* We can give detailed descriptions of states of affairs that our minds cannot even *visualise.* We all remember the picture of the atom that we learned in High School. Tiny electrons orbited around a larger nucleus, in a manner similar to moons orbiting a planet. The only problem with this elegant little model of the atom is that it is completely inaccurate. Electrons, protons and neutrons behave like particles *and* waves.

These 'particles' do not have definite locations and momentums like moons orbiting planets. We are forced to think of the electron as extended throughout the volume of the atom; its influence is spread out, like a wave. By calculating how this 'wave-function' develops, and how it interacts with other 'wave-functions' we can predict the probability of finding the electron in a certain state when we make a measurement. However, when we *measure* the electron we find that it is in a certain state just as if it was a tiny localised particle after all.

Quantum Mechanics has been thoroughly and rigorously tested over many years, and it is a ridiculously successful theory. It is the foundation of modern chemistry and much of modern physics. Different interpretations of Quantum Mechanics emerged as physicists and philosophers tried to explain what on earth is going on. But every interpretation agreed on one point: we cannot use familiar images or experiences to 'picture' the quantum world. The concept is coherent and it explains the evidence; so the theory is accepted as true. So, the moral of the story is we should not let our experiences, or even our imaginations, limit our idea of what is possible.

Aquinas Shows that God Does Not Compute...

Dawkins' conception of God is limited by what we have experienced and what he can imagine. He assumes that a divine intelligence would require a structure similar to a brain's or a computer's. Dawkins' God would be a 'calculating agent', consciously monitoring every particle and taking note of every prayer. It is as if God has to peek at his universe to observe what is happening there and that God's knowledge would amount to an infinitely long list of facts stored up in the divine mind.

If Dawkins had peered into the writings of the great Christian theologians he would have discovered that theists have discussed what God's knowledge could be like, and have concluded that it would be nothing like ours. God would not scrutinize the universe to see what is happening there. God does not go through the processes of making computations and calculations to discover answers. God is not physical, and he already knows everything that is true.

But how can this be? How can God know *anything*, nevermind *everything*, if God does not have a brain? The theologian and philosopher Thomas Aquinas[27] gave a detailed answer. Aquinas knew that human knowledge depends on our brains; we are embodied knowers. Yet God's knowledge cannot be the result of any physical process as God is not physical in any way. So what, Aquinas wondered, explained God's knowledge?

To Aquinas, God's knowledge would be like our knowledge of our own feelings and our own state of mind. We have self-awareness. If I drop a bowling ball on your toe, you will not need to 'work out' that it hurts. You will be directly aware that you are in pain, simply because you are conscious. You simply know what you're feeling and thinking because you are self-aware. You don't *infer* that you are feeling pain by observing the

---

[27] The discussion of Aquinas draws on Brian Davies '*An Introduction to the Philosophy of Religion*' (Oxford:2004), 191–7.

fact that you are leaping up and down, holding your left foot and shouting 'ouch!'

Be careful not to identify your consciousness with your brain states.[28] If I measured everything that happened in your brain after I dropped the bowling ball, and then described the effect this had on your nervous system, I would not have given a good description of your pain. I would have left something important out: *what it felt like for you to be in pain*. I would not have described your conscious experience. At most conscious experience is something that is *produced* by the brain; it is not identical with the brain.

As it happens, *you* might not be able to give this feeling of pain a precise definition. It might prove impossible to explain in words how this particular ache differs from the feeling you get when you stub your toe on a doorstep. *You* will still know the difference. You might not be able to find the exact words to express your anger. Most likely, you will be content to scream and kick me. Sometimes we can put what we experience into words or propositions. On many other occasions, we have difficulty describing what we have felt, even in art and poetry.

We also have 'know-how'—things we can do without thinking about it. Know-how includes skills like the ability to run, or to throw a ball. And this is important—we quite often cannot put our know-how into words. It would be difficult to write out a list of specific step-by-step instructions that could tell someone how to balance on one leg, never-mind how to kiss. There are some things that cannot be learned from a book.

Now, God would know what he is capable of doing, and his 'know how' would include his ability to create anything

---

[28] Many thinkers argue that there must be more to the human mind than the brain and its functions. Recently the case has been advanced by Stewart Goetz and Charles Taliaferro in *'Naturalism'* (Eerdmans:2008) and *'A Brief History of the Soul'* (Wiley-Blackwell:2011); and in the collection of essays edited by Mark Baker and Stewart Goetz *'The Soul Hypothesis'* (Continuum:2011).

that can be sensibly described. By having self-awareness God would be immediately conscious of everything that is possible. Moreover, we shouldn't picture God's 'know-how' as an infinite list of 'things I can do' stored somewhere in God's mind. It would be like our immediate and intuitive knowledge of how we are feeling. We can put some of this knowledge into words and propositions. But we'd never be able to put it all in a list.

God's knowledge would also include knowledge of everything that he has decided to create and keep in existence. And, as Aquinas reminds us, *everything that isn't God has been created by God. God would know everything about this universe because he created it and sustains everything in it.* He would not know anything by working out a solution or taking a look at the world. Once we remember that God is maximally powerful, we can see that God would know everything that is true, *all at once*, just by knowing himself and what he has created.

Aquinas does not provide us with a definitive proof of what God must be like. He only presents one possibility. However, he does show that God's knowledge would be greater and more wonderful than we can fully imagine. He also demonstrates why we should dismiss Dawkins' crude caricature of the divine mind. Aquinas reminds us that we are in God's image, but he is not in ours. Richard Dawkins doesn't believe in a god made in the image of a 21st century technician. Neither did Aquinas; neither did Luther, Wesley, Lewis or Chesterton. The Church Fathers would have been horrified at any attempt to picture God as a 'Big Brain'. It seems that Dawkins is suffering from his own 'God Delusion' for the God he has rejected is a product of his own imagination.

4

Hey—Where's the Evidence?

'On the contrary, Watson, you can see everything. You fail,
however, to reason from what you see. You are too timid in
drawing your inferences.'
  Arthur Conan Doyle, 'The Adventure of the Blue Carbuncle'

For since the creation of the world God's invisible
qualities—his eternal power and divine nature—have been
clearly seen, being understood from what has been made,
so that people are without excuse

'Hey, Religious Believers, Where's the Evidence?'

New Atheist blogger Greta Christina posed this question in
a popular blog post in 2009, confident that believers would not
be able to provide an answer. Greta was concerned that many
religious believers thought that their beliefs were justified if
no one could disprove them. 'Almost nothing can be proved
or disproved with 100 per cent certainty. And proving with
100 per cent certainty that something *doesn't* exist is virtually
impossible'. She helpfully continued

> We don't say, 'Well, you can't prove with 100 per cent
> certainty that the Earth orbits the Sun—it could be a mass
> hallucination caused by a mischievous imp—so we should
> give up on deciding whether it's probably true, and call it a
> matter of personal belief.' With every other kind of claim,
> we accept a standard of reasonable plausibility.[29]

Well, amen to that Greta! It follows that we should not require
the arguments for theism to give us 100% certainty that God
exists. So in the spirit of Greta Christina's criterion of *reasonable
plausibility*, we will evaluate the evidence for God. If theism is
free from inconsistencies and logical flaws, if there is good
evidence supporting it and no strong evidence undermining it,
we should believe that it is true.

But before we get our teeth into the arguments, we should
pause, just to clarify what we mean by 'God'. After all, we
argued in Chapter Two that theism is an 'agent explanation'.
So we need to say a little more about this agent's ability to
bring about the events that we are trying to explain.

Is Theism Fit for Purpose?

Theists define God as the Creator, and therefore the explanation of everything else that exists. However, to believers 'God'
is also a title that is meant to refer to 'the Perfect Being'[30]. Why
do Christians say that God is a 'Perfect being'? They mean that
only God is worthy of worship. If there was a being greater than
God, *it* would be worthy of worship. So, because God is creator
and the Perfect Being, by *definition* God is as good as it gets.

Theists argue that it doesn't make sense to worship a being

---

[29] gretachristina.typepad.com/greta_christinas_weblog/2009/12/wheres-
your-evidence.html Posted on 'Alternet.org/' (Retrieved December 4, 2011).

[30] In this chapter I use 'Perfect Being' theology to *clarify* what theists *mean* by
'God'. I am not advocating an ontological argument. For an introduction
to Perfect Being theology see Thomas V Morris' *Our Idea of God* (IVP:1991).

who is less than personal; so they believe in a perfect *personal* being. Of course this description is often inspired by the theists' religious experiences and traditions. Christians, naturally, turn to the Bible. There God is consistently described as the greatest thing that we can imagine. The book of Ephesians claims that God's love 'surpasses knowledge' and that God can do immeasurably more than we can 'ask or imagine.' So is our idea of God suspect because it is derived from sacred texts?

In 1865 the chemist Friedrich Kekule had a dream; he was beguiled by an image of a snake swallowing its own tail. Kekule was inspired by this idle fancy to propose that the chemical Benzenes had a circular molecular structure. Despite the strange source of inspiration, his model was accepted because it explained the evidence. What inspires a hypothesis is irrelevant. What matters is the hypothesis's capacity to explain the evidence. It does not matter that Christians derive their idea of God from their Scriptures. If this idea is simple, coherent, and if it explains the evidence, it should be taken very seriously indeed.

Theists believe that a perfect being has five characteristics: (i) Perfect Power (ii) Perfect Knowledge (iii) Freedom (iv) Total Independence and (v) Perfect Love. *'Perfect power'* means that God has the power to bring about any state of affairs that can be sensibly described. This 'perfect power' does not include the ability to make illogical actual. The point, rather, is that God's power is as good as it gets; nothing is more powerful than God. *'Perfect knowledge'* simply means that God knows everything that is true of himself and of his creation.

'Freedom' means that God is free to make plans, and that he can act on those plans. That's all it takes to be personal. *'Total independence'* just means that God depends on nothing else for his existence. Nothing else made God, and everything else that exists depends on him. That is to say, nothing made God, and God made everything else. *'Perfect love'* describes God's moral perfection. It is found in God's character.

The greater my freedom, the greater my power, and true

freedom requires choices, knowledge and rationality. The more I know, the greater my options; so perfect power requires perfect knowledge. The point is that God's greatness is unsurpassable; if 'all-powerful' just means that God has the power to do any action that can be sensibly described then it does not mean that God can defy the rules of logic.

God cannot make the three angles of a square circle equal 232, or an ellipse with four sides of equal length. These are meaningless statements; they don't describe things that God cannot do because they do not describe anything. They're just a jangle of words. However, because no external force or power can prevent God doing what he chooses, God's power is perfect.

An unlimited, perfect power would not depend on anything else for its existence; in fact everything else would rely on that power. The unique and unparalleled power of the creator is so great that *everything other than God needs God*. Evil is irrational and chaotic and needlessly destructive. It opposes creation and it is inimical to rationality. A being with perfect power and perfect knowledge could not desire or do evil; God's love and goodness follow from his perfect power and perfect knowledge.

This gives us a very simple description of God: his power is limitless and loving. Of course, our description does not give us a thorough understanding of God's nature. It does not tell us *everything* about God. It says little about *who* God is and *what God has done*; but it does tell us *something* about *what* God is. Our brief description of God's nature is all we need for an astonishingly *simple and powerful* hypothesis. One being who can be described very simply can explain a vast amount of evidence.

PZ Myer's objects that theism's unscientific nature makes it a meaningless hypothesis:

> The nature of this god is always vague and undefined and most annoyingly, plastic... any evidence of a deity will be natural, repeatable, measurable, and even observable...

properties which god is exempted from by the believers' own definitions, so there can be no evidence for it.[31]

Myers seems to think that the word 'God' is meaningless because terms like 'all powerful' cannot be mathematically quantified or experimentally tested. But this objection is asinine. We cannot scientifically measure goodness, love, hate, justice, evil, wrong, right, existence, joy, ecstasy, sorrow, knowledge, rationality, mourning, beauty, or anger! Are these all vague, plastic and meaningless concepts? If we had to attach a scientific measurement for every term that we used, all communication would be futile. We have a good grasp of the characteristics of a perfect being; and this is all we need to evaluate theism.

A Brief Briefing on the State of the Design Argument

Over the last two chapters we have built a design argument for the existence of God. We have noted that the universe obeys laws of nature; laws that science cannot ultimately explain. And we have noted that our world has surprisingly complex and remarkable creatures. We know from our own experience, and from observing others, that minds create purpose and order. Agents compose essays, plan buildings and produce masterpieces. So it seems reasonable to suppose that a mind can explain the vast array of complex order that we see, both in the living world and in the wider universe. Of course, this mind needs enough power to impose order on the universe.[32]

Incredibly, some sceptics argue that we are wrong to be amazed at the order we observe in our universe. If there was no complex order in our universe we couldn't exist. And if we didn't

---

[31] Read Myers unintentionally hilarious foray into philosophical theology: scienceblogs.com/pharyngula/2010/10/its_like_he_was_reading_my_mind.php (retrieved 1st July 2011).

[32] 'Cosmological and Design Arguments' Richard Gale & Alexander Pruss in *The Oxford Handbook of the Philosophy of Religion* Wainwright ed. 2005.

exist, no one would be around to marvel at all the complex order in the universe. So, maybe we shouldn't be surprised to discover that our universe has the right ingredients for life; if it didn't we wouldn't be here to observe it! But this confuses two very different ideas. It confuses sentence (A) *If human observers exist, it is inevitable that they will observe an ordered universe* with sentence (B) *it is inevitable that human observers exist.* (A) makes sense, but (B) is just crazy. Given all the ways our universe *could* have turned out, our existence is extremely unlikely.

But at this point the atheist can reply: 'Ah! Have you considered that if we give an infinite amount of monkeys an infinite number of typewriters and an infinite amount of time, sooner or later one will produce the complete works of Shakespeare by accident? So, if we live in an infinitely large universe, then sooner or later order was bound to emerge, just by chance, in some region or other. So we shouldn't be surprised at the appearance of design. We just happen to live in a part of the universe with enough order for the existence of observers!'

This reply seems very weak.[33] Suppose our universe is infinitely large. We still have to ask 'is this infinite universe governed by design or chance?' So imagine two infinite universes, one created by God and one governed by chance. Which universe will contain more complex order? Obviously, the universe which God governs! While a small fraction of an infinite universe governed by chance will be ordered, the greater part will be chaotic. A universe governed by God would be ruled by a rational and creative agent, so it will be characterised by order, and contain many more examples of apparent design.

The more complex order we observe, the greater the probability that we live in a universe which has been designed. A small region of order is all that is required for the existence

---

[33] Lydia McGrew points out weaknesses in the 'many-universes' response to the design argument from Fine-Tuning in 'Likelihoods, Multiple Universes, and Epistemic Context.' *Philosophia Christi* 7 (2005): 475–81.

of humans; but we do not observe a small sea of regularity surrounded by an ocean of chaos; we observe an abundance of order wherever we look. So, even if our universe is infinitely large, our observations support theism and not atheism.

The atheist's appeal to an infinite universe was suspicious in any case: any surprising fact could be explained this way. In an infinite universe governed by chance, *every physically possible event occurs sooner or later.* If a message formed in the clouds stating 'God exists. Repent and believe the Gospel!' the atheist could simply reply 'well, the universe is vast, maybe infinitely so. So sooner or later, on some planet or other, clouds were bound to take on that shape!' And if you visited a zoo to find a monkey typing out the works of Shakespeare you would conclude that one of the infinite numbers of typewriting monkeys dispersed throughout the infinite universe had finally gotten lucky.

Getting Personal about Right and Wrong

The existence of God is a controversial topic, so let's state a proposition that everyone can agree on—'It is always wrong to torture infants to death purely for fun.' That's a statement about morality, and I'll assume that everyone reading this book agrees with the statement. (If you don't you need to put this book down and seek psychiatric help very quickly.) However we can disagree over what makes that statement true.

Theism provides an excellent explanation for human morality. The statement 'it is wrong to torture babies to death for fun' expresses two things. It expresses a rule: 'Don't torture babies!' But it also expresses a value: innocent human life is precious and worthy of protection. Human life is not a disposable good and we cannot use human beings any way we like. The rule ('don't torture babies') is based on the value ('innocent human life is precious'). Without the value the rule has no foundation.

Moral rules are based on the deep value and significance of each individual human life. Most cultures describe human life as sacred. We do not just protect human life; we prohibit stealing from and lying about other humans. Nearly every culture has some concept of theft and murder. It is interesting that every functioning culture has taboos concerning the *procreation* of human life. Rules about adultery and incest abound.

Social enculturation and genetic hardwiring might explain why we feel *as if* we have moral obligations. But not one of these scientific accounts can tell us if we *really have* moral obligations. Is it *really true* that we have an obligation to protect innocent life? Or is this belief a useful fiction—a by-product of evolving nervous systems? There are scientific and political theories that attempt to show how moral rules benefit the human race. But not one of these theories can tell us if an innocent human life *really is precious*, or if it just *seems to be precious*.

But we can't make sense of our world of experience without a strong belief in moral realities. We experience moral outrage or personal guilt when we believe that moral rules are broken. Most of us are committed to the existence of moral rules and values. Even the worst psychopath offers an excuse for his actions ('I couldn't help my rage/I was only following orders'). We seem unable to live our lives believing that morality is a fiction.

So it seems that we need to explain the existence of moral rules that protect human life. Now these rules express *values*. So what gives each human individual such immense value? Values don't reside in electrons and they're not caused by the Strong Nuclear Force. Nearly all of our moral beliefs seem to be based on the value of the person. But if human beings are the unintended, inconsequential by-product of an impersonal universe then it is difficult to see why we would place *any* substantial value on an individual person. Many humans might *like* the idea of being intrinsically valuable. But so what? Why should their opinion trump the opinion of the sociopath or the tyrant?

Of course if God exists, he is the cause of everything else. That makes God the most valuable thing that exists. God is *personal.* And this goes some way to explaining the tremendous value of each individual human person. Part of the reason God is great is because he is rational and free. So we *resemble* the greatest thing in existence—God—in important ways. And our personal nature means that we can *enter into a relationship* with God—because he is personal too.

Furthermore we have significance because we were *planned.* We have a great value because we are significant to God. If atheism is true we are unplanned and are thus insignificant. If theism is true we have immense significance because the being who brought the Cosmos into being values us, made us to be like him, and can enter into a relationship with us. So theism can account for the objective moral value of each human in a way that atheism cannot.

The Moral of Morality

British Law is seldom praised for its common sense, but in 2008 the Daily Telegraph revealed my country's most ridiculous rule. Although it is not a criminal offence, there is a legal ban on dying in Parliament. This is proscribed because the Palace of Westminster is a Royal Palace, and anyone who dies in a Royal Palace is entitled to a state funeral. This rule is absurd. How would the courts punish a corpse? Would there be some sort of fine? And how could we ensure that it received a fair trial?

There are more absurd laws that authorities ignore. It is illegal to eat a mince pie on Christmas Day; but the police have yet to stop the practice. It is treason to place a postage stamp with the Queen's image upside down; yet no one in living memory has been prosecuted under that law.[34] There is a general principle that humans recognize as binding. We should not be required to obey rules that are pointless or absurd.

---

[34] www.telegraph.co.uk/news/uknews/1568475/Ten-stupidest-laws-are-named.html. The BBC claims, 'Some of the laws did exist but have since been overturned.' www.bbc.co.uk/news/magazine-17610820.

Now consider the universe according to PZ Myers:

> The universe is a nasty, heartless place where most things wouldn't mind killing you if you let them. No one is compelled to be nice; you or anyone could go on a murder spree, and all that is stopping you is your self-interest (it is very destructive to your personal bliss to knock down your social support system) and the self-interest of others, who would try to stop you.[35]

We all seek good purposeful lives because we want to make a moral difference. In fact, we believe that we are *obligated* to seek such lives. We believe that we *ought* to aim at making the world a better place. But, as we said above, we can't be required to engage in an activity if that activity is pointless or self-defeating. So how do we explain our obligation to live a good life in a heartless and nasty universe?

There is no guarantee that we can have a good and meaningful life in a universe that is purposeless and pointless. We are usually uncertain about the consequences of our moral actions. We give to charity, but we often don't know what difference this will make. We try to be honest and to have integrity in our actions. But we never know for sure if this makes the world a more enjoyable place for us and those we love. Maybe we're just providing opportunities for the dishonest and the conniving to get ahead. How can we tell if our moral actions *matter*?

Perhaps morality benefits humanity's survival prospects. Morality certainly makes us *feel* noble and significant. Those are good reasons to be moral. But we might have equally good reasons to ignore our moral feelings. There are times when it might be in our interests *not* to be moral. So why *must* we be moral when we can get away with immorality? Why should the humanity of those living in Somalia or Tibet override my

---

[35] scienceblogs.com/pharyngula/2009/08/morality_doesnt_equal_god.php (retrieved 16th April 2012).

nation's long term interests? Why should my nation's long term interests override my short term political ambitions?

How could we be *obligated* to live moral lives in PZ Myer's universe? There are, after all, perfectly reasonable alternatives. The philosopher Susan Wolf,[36] in a famous paper 'Moral Saints', suggested that a life of virtue is unattractive. Moral perfection is not a sensible goal, in Wolf's opinion. A morally perfect person values other individuals at least as much as they love themselves. Moral Saints spend their time feeding the poor and helping the homeless. They do not have the time to develop their culinary skills, or the cash to visit the finest restaurants. Saints attempt to be inoffensive and nice. They cannot develop Paul Newman's cool or Oscar Wilde's wit.

We want life to be varied and interesting—and Saints are dull. It is better to strive for an interesting life, then, than a moral life. It is better, by far, to be Jack Nicholson on 'Letterman' than Maximilian Kolbe in Auschwitz.[37] If our moral feelings are the result of evolution's purposeless process, and if we have no guarantee that trying to be moral makes the world better, what exactly is wrong with Wolf's argument? Why can't we value our personal tastes more than we value the well-being of others?

For the theist these objections to morality don't even make sense. Yes, there is more to life than morality. Yes, we can be very grateful that Paul Newman made 'The Hustler' (and he was good in 'Butch Cassidy and the Sundance Kid' too). But we live in a moral universe with God at its centre. Whenever we make a moral choice we do something *intrinsically* valuable because we are doing something that God sees and values.

It is absurd to demand that someone achieve the impossible. So, if there is no guarantee that our efforts to make a moral

---

[36] Susan Wolf's classic article 'Moral Saints' can be read in an anthology edited by Louis P Pojman *Ethical Theory: Classical and Contemporary Readings*.

[37] Incarcerated in a concentration camp, Fr. Kolbe voluntarily took the place of a fellow prisoner who had been condemned to death by starvation.

difference can succeed, we are not obligated to live a moral life. The only way we can have such a guarantee is if our lives have a purpose in a meaningful universe. We need to know that we are part of a plan, and a personal cause of our universe and our lives is necessary to produce such a plan. So if we believe that we are genuinely obligated to seek a good life we should believe in God. To put that another way, the existence of God explains why we *ought* to be good, and why moral rules are binding.[38]

Morality and the appearance of design are explained if we live in a universe that has been created by a God of unlimited power and love. But Christian Theism is much more than a philosophical system. Christianity doesn't just claim that God is the ultimate explanation for the order and existence of our universe. The Christian theist believes that God is the meaning of life; God is the most desirable thing, the greatest good. So theism should make sense of our deepest longings. Can God satisfy our spiritual desires?

To answer that question we will need more than philosophical proofs and religious experiences. We will need some reason to believe that God has revealed himself to us. In this chapter we argued that we have good evidence *that* God is real and we said something about *what* God is (unlimited power and love). In our final chapters we will ask if we can know *who* God is. We'll begin by asking if the life of Jesus can give us an answer.

---

[38] For discussions of the moral argument see J. Wall and D. Baggett *Good God: The Theistic Foundations of Morality* (Oxford:2011); W. Wainwright's *Religion and Morality* (Ashgate:2005); J. Hare's *God and Morality* (Blackwell:2006).

5

Whales, Tall Tales, and Miracles

There is but one God, the Father, from whom all things came and for whom we live; and there is but one Lord, Jesus Christ, through whom all things came and through whom we live.

Turn to me and be saved, all the ends of the earth! For I am God, and there is no other. By myself I have sworn; from my mouth has gone out in righteousness a word that shall not return: 'To me every knee shall bow, every tongue shall swear allegiance.'

Jesus is 'the stone you builders rejected, which has become the cornerstone.' Salvation is found in no one else, for there is no other name under heaven given to mankind by which we must be saved.

Therefore God exalted him to the highest place and gave him the name that is above every name, that at the name of Jesus every knee should bow, in heaven and on earth and under the earth, and every tongue acknowledge that Jesus Christ is Lord, to the glory of God the Father.

In 1861 boats from the whaler *The Star of the East* chased down a huge Sperm whale near the Falkland Islands, and put a harpoon in the behemoth's side. The beast was in no hurry to die; as the crews closed in to finish off their prey, she lifted nearly ten tonnes of tail out of the water and brought it down on the lead boat. It disintegrated, smashed into infinitesimal fragments, and its occupants were scattered. The harpooner, James Bartley, was tossed a dozen feet into the air, and then plunged deep into ice cold Antarctic waters.

Bartley struggled to return to the surface, but the shock of the freezing temperature numbed his limbs. The sheer violence of the whale's death throes had turned the water into bloody foam; he found it difficult to navigate through the maelstrom. He managed to swim for a few meters before he realised he was making a horrible, deadly error. He was swimming towards the gaping mouth of the whale. Still underwater, he attempted to regain his bearings, and to strike for a safer spot on the surface. But the ocean turned dark. He could dimly perceive the huge maw that had surrounded him. Paralysed with fear, yet fully conscious, James Bartley was swallowed alive.

The whalers on the other boat were unaware of Bartley's fate. Failing to find their friend, they assumed he had drowned. The second whaling boat dragged the dead whale back to *The Star of the East*, and began to strip the whale down to the bone before the gathering sharks could feast on the carcass. It was late in the day and the whale men hurried at their task. They began by gutting the corpse and ripping out the whale's stomach; and out tumbled James Bartley, screaming like a new-born child. He had been bleached white by the stomach acids, and driven half mad by terror. But Bartley was alive. Furthermore, he recovered to achieve fame as 'a second Jonah'. His case caused a sensation in the English medical establishment. He was a living, breathing miracle.

Or at least he would have been if this story was true. But, however much we might want to believe this horror story, it is pure legend.[39] Medical records of the era do not mention a Mr Bartley, or anyone else, suffering from burns caused by stomach acids. A tale like this did make its way into the *New York Times* in 1896, but the paper was merely repeating a story that a journalist claimed to have read in the *Yarmouth Mercury*. Alas, the *Mercury* records no such incident; but it does mention that a whale ran ashore at Gorleston, just south of great Yarmouth. This inspired many tall tales in the vicinity. But crucially, no whaler named *The Star of the East* operated in the late 19th Century; and whaling off the Falkland Islands did not commence until 1909.

The Times succeeded in creating a legend. Christian apologists believed that this tale vindicated the story of Jonah; everyone else was mesmerised because this story taps into our primal fear of being devoured alive. But simple fact-checking proves the story was false. It survived and thrived because it was told thousands of miles away from where it was said to have taken place, and because this is the sort of story we want to believe.

A Brief History of the Historical Jesus

There are plenty of tall tales in the world, and we've all been taken in by one at some time or other. Christians, according to the sceptic, make the mistake of basing an entire religion on the Easter legend. What New Atheists find particularly offensive is Christians asserting that there is good historical evidence for this myth. It's one thing to be taken in by a good yarn; that's pitiable. But to insist that everyone else has a *rational duty to believe* your bunk is beyond contempt. New Atheists simply cannot take Christians insisting that the Resurrection of Jesus Christ is one of the best attested facts of ancient history.

Many Christian historians argue that *three facts* are indisputable: (1) *Jesus' closest followers believed that they had seen*

---

[39] See Edward B. Davis, 'A Whale of a Tale: Fundamentalist Fish Stories' www. asa3.org/ASA/PSCF/1991/PSCF12-91Davis.html.

Jesus several days after the Crucifixion; (2) that *these same witnesses believed that Jesus' body had been resurrected*; and (3) that *the first Christians confirmed that Jesus' tomb was empty*. Now the sceptic needs a good explanation for those three facts. And the Christian alleges that the atheist does not have one, whereas the belief of the Early Church does neatly explain the data: Jesus really did rise from the dead. Or to put that another way, the first Christian's faith in the Resurrection was based on facts and hard evidence. It was not the result of strange, spiritual experiences or a leap of faith.

Most sceptics assume that we can dismiss Jesus' resurrection just as easily as we can dismiss James Bartley's passage through a whale's digestive system. Surely this is a story that was invented long after Jesus' death to bring spiritual comfort to Jesus' followers? It is nothing more than a pious 'tall tale'. In fact, aren't all the stories in the Gospels somewhat suspect? Didn't the first Christians simply invent tales about Jesus that had no connection to reality?

That attitude could have been taken seriously in the first half of the twentieth century. Prominent scholars, like Rudolph Bultmann, argued that the Gospels could tell us a lot about the Churches who invented these stories, but nothing much about Jesus himself. These critics assumed that the first Christians had no method for preserving reliable information about Jesus; and in any case the first Christians did not try to remember accurate information about Jesus. If a story would help Jesus' movement grow, Christians felt justified in inventing it.

But from the 1950's onward, confidence in the Gospels general reliability grew. Scholars noticed that the Gospels included a lot of information that the Church was unlikely to invent—for example Peter's denial and Judas' treachery. It is also remarkable that the Gospels say very little about the issues that vexed the earliest Churches. The first Christian communities were bitterly divided over relationships between Jewish and Gentile Christians. Yet Jesus says nothing about circumcision.

He says very little about Gentiles, and how Gentiles should treat the Old Testament law. If the early Church was in the habit of inventing stories, why did it not settle these disputes by fabricating a parable or two?

The Gospels address issues that were irrelevant to the gentiles joining the Churches in droves. Why invent teachings about the Temple tax, or about forgiving your brother before you offer a sacrifice? Why include a prophecy that tells Christians living near Jerusalem how to act in the face of an impending Roman invasion? These passages became completely irrelevant after the Roman-Jewish war and the destruction of the Temple in AD70. It only makes sense to include these stories in your Gospel if you are trying to preserve information about Jesus. And sociology teaches us that groups like the first churches generally do everything that they can to preserve information about their founder.

So we do not find evidence of creative storytelling where we would expect to find it. But we know that memorisation was an important part of Jewish education, and especially the education of a Rabbi's disciples. If Jesus' students followed the customs of their day, they would have memorised many of their master's teachings. The Gospels were written within a generation of Jesus' death—so these eyewitnesses could be consulted. We know that eyewitnesses, like the Twelve and Mary of Magdala, were highly esteemed in the Early Church.[40] We also know the mother Church at Jerusalem had some authority in the first decades of Church growth. So there was a 'check' on the types of story that could circulate about Jesus.

[40] Richard Bauckham's *Jesus and the Eyewitnesses* (Eerdmans: 2008) and Ben Witherington's *What Have they Done With Jesus* (HarperOne:2007) develop the case that the Gospels contain eyewitness testimony. Witherington notes the importance of key eyewitnesses like James, Peter, Mary and the 'Beloved Disciple' in the early Church. Bauckham notes that Papias, a first Century Bishop, preferred the testimony of living eyewitnesses to written texts; this illustrates the importance of eyewitnesses in early Christianity.

Scholars have long noticed that many passages in Matthew, Luke and Mark are similar, and some are identical. Most scholars believe that Matthew and Luke wrote after Mark, and used Mark as one of their sources. Whatever the case, it is certain that a deal of copying went on. This shows that the Gospel writers used their sources *carefully*—so much so that they could copy sections word for word. The first Christians had the motivation to keep their memories of Jesus intact, they had the means for accessing good information about Jesus, and the evidence is that they were trying to faithfully preserve his memory.

So sceptics cannot dismiss every story recorded in the Gospels as a tall tale. *At least* some of the information in the Gospels accurately reflects the life of Jesus.[41] So what about our three facts? Are they tall tales or solid truths? Let's start with fact (1) *Some of Jesus' closest followers believed that they had seen Jesus several days after the Crucifixion.* The Crucifixion of Jesus is attested outside the New Testament by historians like Tacitus. And Crucifixion was such a scandalous way to die that it is absurd to suppose that any group would *pretend* that their leader had been crucified! Consider the most loathsome criminal known to you. That is how people felt about the victims of crucifixion in the Ancient World.

We know of 'messianic' types who tried to found movements in this period. Theudas claimed that he would part the waters of the Jordan; an Egyptian who said that he would cause the walls of Jerusalem to come tumbling down. Would-be kings like the shepherd Athronges or John of Gischala. In each case Rome executed the leader; in each case the movement died. So the question arises: 'what was different about Jesus' movement?' The simplest answer is the answer provided by Paul (in 1 Corinthians) and the Gospels. Jesus' followers, on

---

[41] James Dunn explains how Christian communities passed down reliable information in *Jesus Remembered* (Eerdmans: 2003). Craig Keener's *The Historical Jesus of the Gospels* (Eerdmans:2009) explains the importance of memorisation in ancient Mediterranean education.

the basis of eyewitness reports, believed that their leader had returned from the dead.

There is nothing extraordinary about fact (1). Sceptics enthusiastically point out that people can have all kinds of visions and hallucinations. And we need some event to explain the survival of Jesus' movement. So there is a strong consensus that (1) is true. Noted scholar Maurice Casey states 'I conclude that the evidence for early appearances, from the women to St Paul, is unimpeachable, but we should not believe in the literal truth of the resurrection stories.'[42] And, as you can tell from the last half of that sentence, Casey isn't exactly sympathetic to the case for the Resurrection.

'There are a lot of tall tales going about the world...'

So why does Casey believe that the Resurrection didn't happen? Casey believes in the 'legendary development hypothesis'. Initially the first Christians, including Paul, believed that Jesus' spirit had survived crucifixion. Religious visions convinced them that Jesus' spirit was alive and well with God in heaven. But over time the stories became exaggerated. As Christianity spread into the Gentile world, Christians began to tell taller and taller tales about their Lord, until Christians came to believe that Jesus' body rose from the dead. Pious legends developed and the doctrine of Jesus' resurrection was born.

This sounds like a plausible theory; the only problem with it is that it can't explain away the facts. Gentile culture wasn't happy with the idea of bodily resurrection. Greek philosophy tended to think that the body was an impediment to spiritual development. Jews, however, believed that the body was good because it belonged to God, and they looked forward to the resurrection of their bodies on Judgment day. But the legendary

---

[42] James Crossley and Maurice Casey present a scholarly case against the resurrection of Jesus in *How Did Christianity Begin* Michael Bird and James Crossley (SPCK: 2008).

development hypothesis asks us to believe that Jewish Christians first believed that Jesus only spiritually survived the cross; then Greek and gentile Christians hijack this idea to promote a physical resurrection. This is wildly implausible.

Then there's that odd word—'resurrection'.[43] Paul clearly teaches that Jesus was 'resurrected'. We know from Galatians that Paul's message had the approval of the mother church in Jerusalem. 1 Corinthians cites Peter and the Twelve as witnesses to this resurrection. And the Corinthian Christians all believed in *Jesus'* resurrection; they just didn't want to believe that *they* would be resurrected one day. They were looking forward to escaping from their bodies. But Paul argued that the Corinthians were going to have to get used to the idea. They *already* believed, with the apostles, that Jesus had risen bodily from the grave; therefore they should believe that *they too* would rise bodily from the dead.

You see the word 'resurrection' could only mean one thing in Jewish thought. It meant bodily rising from the grave to be judged by God. You could no more have a 'spiritual' resurrection than a 'square triangle' or a 'married bachelor'. Paul referred the Corinthians to the traditions that he and the other Apostle's had passed on from the Churches inception. And the message of those traditions was that Jesus had risen bodily from the grave, been accepted by his father, and that he was now at the Father's right hand.

Of course Jews were not expecting anyone to be resurrected until judgment day, when all the faithful would rise from the grave. Then God would create the New Heavens and New Earth. No-one was expecting one person to be resurrected on his own before the end of the world! So why on earth did the first

---

[43] The Jewish concept of resurrection is described in texts like 1 Enoch 51; Daniel 12; 2 Maccabees 7:11, 2 Baruch 49-51; Josephus War 3.374f; Josephus Apion 2.218; Wisdom of Solomon 3, 9:15; Syballine Oracles 4.179-92; The Apocalypse of Moses 41.2f, 43.2f; Isaiah 26:19

Christians conclude that Jesus had been resurrected? A mere vision of Jesus might have led the disciples to believe that Jesus' 'angel' was visiting them, or that Jesus' soul was waiting with God. They might even have convinced themselves that God had transformed Jesus into a star, or had translated him into the heavenly realm. But something led Jesus' Jewish followers to believe that he had been resurrected. It is difficult to explain what would convince them of this—unless it had actually happened.

'...the worst of it is that some of them are true.'[44]

So is the 'legendary development' hypothesis dead? Not quite. The New Testament scholar James Crossley has no quarrel with facts 1&2. However, he argues that the Empty Tomb is a legend. The first disciples based their belief in the Resurrection on their visions of Jesus and little else. No one checked to see if Jesus' body was still in the ground. The empty tomb was not proclaimed by the first Christians in Jerusalem. As a matter of fact, Jesus body might never have made it to a tomb—he might have been buried in a common grave.

Then, as Christianity grew, people wanted to know where and how Jesus had been buried, who discovered that the body was missing and so forth. So the early Church indulged in a bit of creative story telling. It claimed that Jesus had been buried in Joseph of Arimathea's tomb, and then fabricated a story about a group of women discovering this tomb was empty. According to Mark's Gospel, the same women were so scared by an angelic messenger that they forgot to tell the other disciples about their discovery, and that the tomb was empty.[45] The story of the discovery of Jesus' empty tomb is a fiction, creatively invented by the Church decades after the events of the first Easter.

---

[44] Winston Churchhill said this—or so I've heard.

[45] Many critical scholars believe that Mark's Gospel originally ended at 16:8, without a resurrection appearance. Yet there is no doubt: Mark clearly believed in the physical resurrection of Jesus, and knew of resurrection appearances: Mark 8:31–33; 9:9, 30–32; 10:32–34 & 16:6.

This stretches credibility to breaking point. The reader must assume that the women told someone about their discovery, as Mark knows about it. Luke and John clearly understand Mark to mean that the women passed their story on to the disciples, but then failed to proclaim Jesus' resurrection publicly. That seems to be a saner reading of Mark 16:1-8. And why would the Church invent this particular story? Granted, women were important to the first Churches. But a woman's testimony would not be taken seriously by outsiders; it had no value in court. It would have been tremendously embarrassing to admit that the first witnesses to the events of Easter were women!

If this story is an invention of early apologists we have to ask why they were so extraordinarily incompetent. A child could have created a story that would have been easier to sell! Why not invent a story in which a male follower visited Jesus' burial place, to be told by an angel not to mention this empty tomb to anyone in case they should be tempted to worship there? Why not spin a tale, in which Jesus was buried in a common grave with the poor, to fulfil the Scriptures? In fact, there seems to be very good sermon material in such a story. The poor were buried in unmarked patches of land. Losing track of Jesus' burial place would have been understandable in such circumstances. The shame of a pauper's burial was nothing compared to the shame of Crucifixion; and unlike the story of Jesus' honourable burial by a member of the Sanhedrin, this story would have been difficult to verify.

Finally, Matthew's Gospel has to respond to the charge that the disciples stole Jesus' body. Now grave robbing was associated with witchcraft, so this was a serious accusation. Matthew would not have included it in his Gospel lightly. This seems to have been the standard Jewish response to the Easter message, and Matthew cannot ignore it. Even so, it is interesting to see what Jew and Christian were agreed on. Both parties agree that Jesus was buried in Joseph of Arimathea's tomb. They agree that disciples were at the tomb on Easter morning. And they agree that this tomb was empty. And we would expect Jesus' friends and enemies to check on the status of his body. And, by itself, there is nothing miraculous about a missing body. This is not a claim that requires extraordinary evidence.[46]

The Last Myth-Makers

So if we can safely conclude that Jesus' followers had experiences of his presence after his death, we can also safely conclude that Jesus' tomb was inspected and found to be empty. We also know that the experiences were of a risen body. From the very beginning Jesus was said to be 'resurrected'. If the Church was in the habit of inventing stories it had a wider range of concepts to draw on; and the Church could have invented a story that was impossible to falsify. They could have preached that Jesus' spirit was yet alive at the Father's right hand, and that he would be reunited with his body on the last day, when God would proclaim him Messiah. It would have been impossible for Jesus' enemies to prove such a message was wrong. Instead the first Christians preached a message that could have been overturned by the discovery of a corpse.

So sceptics have to explain three inconvenient truths. (1) *Jesus' closest followers believed that they had seen Jesus several days after the Crucifixion*; (2) that *these followers believed that Jesus' body had been resurrected*; and (3) that *the first Christians confirmed that Jesus' tomb was empty*. The sceptic must explain these three facts, and he must do so without recourse to conspiracy theories. These abounded in the seventeenth and eighteenth centuries.

[46] Matthew's report that the dead left the tombs at Jesus' death is sometimes taken as evidence that Matthew was a poor historian given to creative story telling. But we need to compare Matthew's Passion to Josephus' account of the signs that accompanied the fall of the Temple, or Dio Cassius' account of Claudius' death. These are wilder tales by far. Yet no one writes off all of their material on the Temple's fall or the Emperor's death! We should also note that Luke's account is more subdued, and contains little that could count as legendary embellishments.

One scholar explained the feeding of the 5,000 as an elaborate magic trick; Jesus conspired with Essenes, who hid in caves, handing out loaves as Jesus required them. Jesus' simulated walking on water by placing planks just below the surface. Jesus didn't mean to say 'be calm' to the storm; he was addressing the disciples. As luck would have it, at that very moment, the storm calmed down.

In the 19th Century David Strauss tore such theories out of the history books. Strauss did not believe that Jesus had performed any miracles. He insisted that the miracle stories were myths that developed over successive retellings of the life of Jesus. But to Strauss' mind explanation by a conspiracy theory was no more plausible than an explanation by a miracle. The 'just so' stories produced by rationalist theologians were as improbable as any miracle. Serious scholarship has never again conjured up the nonsense that Strauss decisively refuted.

Some complain that we do not have an 'eyewitness' document which describes the Resurrection. Only this sort of primary source should be taken seriously by historians; or so the argument goes. Historians, on this view, should just go through eyewitness accounts and stroke out what seems unreliable. What is left is history. This is ill-informed nonsense. As if the discovery of a first century document in Palestine, saying 'I, Mary of Magdala, witnessed the Resurrected Christ' would somehow improve the case for the Resurrection! This wouldn't even tell us something we didn't already know—that Mary believed that she had witnessed the Resurrected Christ.[47]

If we were to follow the New Atheist's methodology, most of ancient history would find its way to the wastepaper basket. The New Atheist is advocating what Roger Collingwood called

---

[47] In any case, we do have an eyewitness account, Paul's first letter to the Corinthians. Some sceptics try to make hay out of the fact that Paul does not mention the empty tomb in 1 Corinthians. But Paul doesn't mention Caiaphas or Pilate either. Does that mean he didn't know about them?

a 'scissors and paste' approach to history. Christian historians are not abandoning critical history by inferring events which are not described in their sources. Philosopher of history Mark Day makes this clear:

> The key to critical history is not so much that one *excludes* testimony, as that one reasons from the evidence to produced statements about the past that are *in addition* to anything testified. The historian includes in their account passages which cannot be found in any source.[48]

So there are three points we need to make here. The first is that we have already noted that the Gospels should not be treated as a collection of myths; the second is that there is nothing miraculous about an empty tomb, a vision of a religious leader, or a claim that someone rose from the dead. We should be clear that the tomb was empty and that the disciples believed that Jesus had been resurrected. And this brings us to the third point that we need to make. The sceptic cannot use conspiracy theories to explain the evidence. No ridiculous stories about women visiting the wrong tomb, and confusing a gardener for their Messiah. No tall tales about Jesus' family removing his body to the family plot, and forgetting to mention this to his disciples. No fantasies in which Jesus' disciples steal his body to start a world religion! And in the absence of old fashioned conspiracy theories, we are left with one explanation: Christianity is correct. Jesus rose from the dead.

Beyond the Grave, Beyond Personality

Jesus' ministry and Resurrection had an extraordinary effect on his first followers. Paul's letters were written within a generation of Jesus' Crucifixion. He uses formulae, prayers

---

[48]   *The Philosophy of History* (Continuum:2008), 18. It is also worth reading John Tosh's *The Pursuit of History* (Longman:2009) and Richard Evans' *In Defence of History* (Granta:2001) .

and confessions that his readers would approve of. This is the language of the first Jewish Christians. A study of these early Christian devotional practices shows that the first Christians worshipped Jesus. This is incredible as Jewish monotheists believed that religious worship should be given to YHWH and YHWH alone. Yet Jewish Christians confessed Jesus, called upon his name for Salvation, and celebrated a meal at which Jesus was the presiding Lord.[49]

Time and again the New Testament texts casually talk about Jesus as if he has the same authority, power and rights as YHWH. The Old Testament texts, for example, teach us that we must call upon the name of YHWH to be saved (Joel 2:32); Paul reminds the Roman church that they must call on Jesus' name to be saved (Rom. 10:9–13). Isaiah makes clear that every tongue will confess and every knee will bow to YHWH and YHWH alone (Isa. 45:23–5); yet the hymn that Paul quotes in Philippians 2 is clear that every tongue will confess and every knee will bow to Jesus!

YHWH alone walks on the waves and tells the storms to cease (Job 9:8, 38:11; Jonah 1; Ps. 89:9, 107:23–32); yet the early Churches believed that Jesus performed these very miracles. God had a counsel of angels who, many Jews believed, aided him in creation and providence; yet the hymns quoted in Hebrews 2 and Colossians 1 make it clear that Jesus is superior to these

---

[49]   Larry Hurtado gives a summary of the Early Churches' view of Jesus in 'Early Devotion to Jesus: A Report, Reflections and Implications.' *Expository Times* 122/4 (2011): 167–76. See also Hurtado's responses to Dunn and McGrath on his personal blog: larryhurtado.wordpress.com/ The full force of the relevant New Testament texts can be experienced by reading R. Bowman's and JE Komoszewski's *Putting Jesus in His Place* (Kregel:2007).

angelic beings.[50] What God does, from creation to judgment, Jesus does. What God deserves, from praise to obedience, Jesus deserves.

This way of thinking about Jesus permeates the entire New Testament. It is not a product of one Gospel or Paul's theology. As Larry Huratdo concludes:

> amazing devotion to Jesus appeared more like an explosion, a volcanic eruption, than an evolution. However counter-intuitive it will perhaps seem, the exalted claims and the unprecedented devotional practices that reflect a treatment of Jesus as somehow sharing divine attributes and status began among Jewish believers and within the earliest moments of the young Christian movement.

What would cause Jewish monotheists to worship a human being? We can turn to the evidence contained by the Gospels for an answer. Jesus Christ of Nazareth claimed to fulfil all of Israel's hopes; he claimed authority over God's law and God's Temple; he claimed the right to forgive sins and that he would judge the world. In short, Jesus claimed the role reserved for God himself. Yet he also prayed to his Father in Heaven. This was a shocking, bizarre situation, and it would have been easy to dismiss Jesus as another mad prophet, if it were not for the wisdom of his teachings, and *the miracle of the Resurrection.*

It is impossible to overstate how much Jesus changed our conception of God. His followers remained monotheists—they believed in one God. Yet Jesus forced his followers to recognise that God is more than one personality with unlimited power.

---

[50] Ben Witherington III points out that these early hymns to Jesus depend on Jewish 'Wisdom' Theology, and not Greek religious speculation. See *The Indelible Image: Volume II* (IVP Academic: 2010), 118–130. Angels and 'elevated' humans like Enoch often appear in Jewish literature. But not one of these characters receives anything like the praise that the first Churches lavished on Jesus. See the essays in Richard Bauckham's *Jesus and the God of Israel* (Eerdmans:2008).

God is personal, but triune. God is Father, Son and Holy Spirit, three persons, inextricably linked by the same unlimited power and love. As Francis Schaeffer put it, we worship a God who is *infinitely personal*. In the words of CS Lewis, our God is *beyond personality*. Moreover, God became one of us to die like us. Christianity teaches that the Father gave his only Son, who came out of love to suffer to redeem us, and who sends the Spirit to draw us to him.

Compared to this Triune God, who else could be worthy of worship?

6

The Insider Test for Faith

Heaven have mercy on us all - for we are all somehow
dreadfully knocked about the head, and sadly need mending.
                                    Herman Melville, *Moby Dick*

Where can I go from your Spirit?
Where can I flee from your presence?

In April 2000 the historian David Irving was found to be
a Holocaust denier, a racist and an anti-semite by a High
Court Judge. Irving lacked any formal historical training, yet
had earned the grudging respect of many academic historians
with his obsessive pursuit of documents, diaries and witnesses
to illuminate Hitler's conduct during World War Two. Irving
came to wider public attention by writing biographies which
lionised Hitler, and that argued that he was more sinned
against than sinning; in fact Winston Churchill emerged as one
of history's villains in Irving's analysis. Eventually, the logic of
Irving's work led him to deny the reality of the Final Solution.

Irving argued that Hitler never desired the extermination of
Europe's Jews; he wanted Europe's Jews to be exiled to Eastern

Europe. The SS acted against Hitler's orders when it carried out mass executions in Russia. Irving insisted that 'only' a few hundred thousand Jewish civilians perished at the hands of ill-disciplined SS units on the Eastern Front. This number was roughly similar to the number of German civilian causalities caused by the Allied bombing campaign.

It was Irving's contention that there had been no systematic attempt to exterminate Europe's Jews in the gas chambers of Sobibor, Treblinka and other death camps. Those Jews who died in concentration camps died from disease and exposure to the elements. Allied propaganda invented the story of the Holocaust once the conflict was over. Europe's historians had fallen for a Zionist myth. The numerous eyewitnesses to the depravities of the concentration camps were the victims of a 'mass hysteria'.

In 'Denying the Holocaust' (1994) the American historian Deborah Lipstadt outed Irving's neo-facist connections. Lipstadt argued that Irving was one of the 'most dangerous spokespersons for Holocaust denial' because he had earned the respect of many academic historians, and this gave him credibility. She accused Irving of consistently distorting evidence and misquoting sources to exonerate Hitler. Lipstadt further claimed that Irving had been 'discredited' by fellow historians; this might have infuriated Irving more than her other accusations. Whatever his motives, Irving took Lipstadt to High Court for defamation of character.

In court, Irving faced expert witnesses who systematically tore his 'scholarship' to shreds. This was no easy task, as Irving represented himself in court; he proved to be a master of obfuscation and evasion. But inevitably his deliberate falsification of the historical record emerged. Cambridge historian Professor Richard Evans demolished Irving's credibility by painstakingly analysing each source that Irving cited. Irving's self-belief collapsed with his arguments. In his closing statement he addressed the claim that he had connections with European neo-Nazi's. His mind wandered from his prepared notes, and he forgot to address the Judge, Mr Justice Charles Gray, as '*Your Honour.*' Instead, in a surreal slip of the tongue, he called the Judge '*Mein Fuhrer!*'

Mr Justice Gray found in favour of Deborah Lipstadt, rejecting Irving's action in a 350 page judgment that left his academic reputation in ruins. To deny the Holocaust required more than a poor reading of the evidence. It demanded that the historian lie, and lie repeatedly, about the documents and how best to interpret them. Rational argument prevailed at this trial.[51] But the detailed, clinical use of reason made many observers uncomfortable. James Dalrymple commented in the *Independent*:

> I felt like a man in some kind of Kafkaesque dream. What was going on here? Was this some kind of grotesque *Monty Python* episode? Everybody seemed to be in such good spirits. As if they were taking part in some kind of historical parlour game. Spot the gas chamber for 20 points.

Similarly, Phillip Blom wrote in *Berliner Zeitung*:

> ..the debate here was about mass murder, about bizarre arithmetical tasks, that sounded as if they came from a textbook from the gates of Hell: if you have two gassing lorries with a capacity of sixty individuals and you have 172 days to kill 97,000 Jews, how many journeys must each lorry make each day?

Yet Richard Evans needed 'some kind of emotional curtain between the court proceedings and the death camps' to testify effectively. He was not merely protecting his own emotional health. Irving was a powerful orator and a master of sophistry. An emotionally charged courtroom suited Irving, not his

---

[51] The story of Irving's trial is expertly told by Richard Evans in *Telling Lies About Hitler* (Verso:2002) and Deborah Lipstadt, *History on Trial* (Harper:2006).

critics. But the calm recondite atmosphere of the High Court allowed historians like Christopher Browning and Richard Evans to dissect Irving's arguments piece by piece, until the historical credibility of Holocaust denial was in shreds.

It might seem odd to treat belief in God as if it is a 'hypothesis'. Quite often people come to believe in God simply because they feel that someone is expressing himself through creation, rather as an artist does through his writing or painting. And most Christians do not come to faith after considering abstract academic arguments. Christian faith is not a theory; it involves a deep personal repentance before God, and an absolute dependence on Christ. We do not often arrive at such a personal commitment by abstract reasoning alone; more often it results from personal experience. Many come to faith through a profound sense of sin, and an urgent need for forgiveness.

So it might seem odd to have spent five chapters presenting detached, academic reasons for taking belief in God seriously. But New Atheists allege that Christians are in the grip of blind faith. Baptist Pastor turned sceptic John Loftus insists that Christians fail *The Outsider Test:*

> If you were born in Saudi Arabia, you would be a Muslim right now....That is a cold hard fact. Dare you deny it? Since this is so, or at least 99% so, then the proper method to evaluate your religious beliefs is with a healthy measure of skepticism. Test your beliefs as if you were an outsider to the faith you are evaluating. If your faith stands up under muster, then you can have your faith. If not, abandon it...[52]

So, sometimes it is helpful to draw our emotional curtains so that we can assess the evidence with a clear mind. And whatever

---

[52] debunkingchristianity.blogspot.com/2006/02/outsider-test.html (retrieved 1st Jan 2012). Loftus is continually revising the test, and it is not clear which version is 'canonical'.

Mr Loftus's expectations, theism passes his Outsider Test. When we look at the facts dispassionately, we can see that the order of the physical and moral world is best explained by the existence of a personal creator. That seems to be a cold, hard fact, and I dare not deny it. Certainly Mr Loftus has given me no reason to doubt it.

Of course, our social environment has a great deal of influence over our religious, political and moral beliefs. We do not want to uncritically absorb our fundamental beliefs from the society that surrounds us; a little scepticism can, indeed, be helpful. At the same time, we should not be unduly sceptical of our culture's beliefs. If we lived in a different political culture we might not believe that all human beings have intrinsic rights; or we might believe in the intrinsic superiority of our own culture and race. But it would not be sensible to reject liberal democracy because we might have been North Korean!

Nor is it advisable to evaluate every belief from behind emotional curtains; personal experience can provide grounds for many important beliefs. For example, we do not appreciate the value of a human life until we have witnessed childbirth or comforted the dying. And if someone suggested that love and friendship are nothing more than neural and chemical conditions to facilitate bonding, or that beauty was simply an evolved neurological response, we might suggest that he needed to get out of the laboratory a little more, because he simply had not grasped the subject matter.

Now, if there is a God, he is worthy of worship: infinitely loving and morally perfect. So it is likely that a perfect God would want to do more than reveal theological information. Any God worthy of the title would want to engage us, and transform us, by bringing us into relationship with him. As Paul Moser says in *The Evidence for God*:

> A God worthy of worship would not be in the business
> of just expanding our databases or simply giving us

an informational plan of rescue from our troubles. Divine self-revelation...would seek to transform humans motivationally, toward perfect love and its required volitional cooperation with God.[53]

God would not want us to study him from behind emotional curtains; we should expect God to reveal himself in challenging and inspiring ways. The Christian faith claims that God is the ultimate source of meaning and significance; that we were made to know God and to enjoy him forever. So, if Christianity is true it must be existentially relevant, morally challenging, and go some way to satisfying our spiritual needs. Christianity must pass what we could call an 'Insider Test'.

Does religious experience provide evidence for God's existence? And should we trust our own private, personal experiences when reflecting on the Christian faith? Christian theism claims to be much more than an academic explanation of the universe. Theology is not just meant to be studied in the abstract; Christian teaching is meant to be lived. It is meant to enable us to know and to enjoy God. So we need to consider the role of personal experience in coming to faith.

Once More, This Time with Feelings!

Arguably, the phenomenon of religious experience provides additional evidence for theism. After surveying a wide range of evidence from the social sciences, psychologist Michael Argyle reports that

Religious Experiences convey to those who have them a feeling of having been in contact with a powerful force, usually a feeling of unity in the whole of creation, and also of contact with a transcendent being. Those experiencing them have a sense of joy, feel more integrated, perhaps forgiven, have a sense of timelessness, and are convinced

[53] Paul Moser *The Evidence for God* (Cambridge:2010), 17.

that they have been in contact with something real; the experience carries its own validity for them. There are fruits of the spirit in that many who have Religious Experiences want to lead a better life and do more for other people.[54]

Such religious experiences are surprisingly common; many people claim to have discerned God's presence in nature or music; others firmly believe that they have been aware that God has been at work in a sermon or a prayer. Some people are sure that they were unexpectedly and directly aware of God's love, majesty or anger.[55] These were all deep, personal and momentous experiences and they function as a sign of God's existence, just as our moral experiences guide us to believe in the value of love and life.

Intriguingly, there is a common core to many religious experiences—an awareness of something that transcends the natural world, an unexplained personal presence, and a sense that all things are somehow united. This is a good description of a theistic universe—a universe sustained by one, transcendent and personal power. There is a widespread perception that we live, move and have our being in God, and Argyle notes that such experiences are common enough to strengthen the case for God's existence.

If theism is true then God is truly present everywhere, for the entire universe is dependent on God's power. God keeps everything everywhere in existence from one moment to the next. If God is immanent within Creation, as Christians have always insisted, then he is continually revealing himself—just as a musician is present in her musical performances, or as an

---

[54] Michael Argyle *Psychology and Religion* (Routledge:2005), 74

[55] See Montagu Barker's *Psychology, Religion and Mental Health* (Rutherford House: 2000); Charles Taliaferro 'In Defense of the Numinous' in *Philosophy and the Christian Worldview* eds. David Werther and Mark Linville (Continuum, 2012); CS Evans and R. Zachary Manis *Philosophy of Religion* (IVP: 2009), 98-115

artist is revealed in her paintings. We could detect the activity of a divine agent just as we detect the presence of other agents.

However, a word of caution is in order. Perceiving God does not place us in a saving relationship with God. Genesis records that Adam and Eve had profound experiences of God; yet they rebelled against him. The devils are aware of God's holiness, and they despair.[56] I might realise that there is a guitarist in the next classroom when I hear him rehearse; depending on how beautifully (or terribly!) he plays, this might be a deeply emotional experience. *But this experience does not mean that I have a relationship with the guitarist!* So John Calvin warns us:

> ...though experience testifies that a seed of religion is divinely sown in all, *scarcely one in a hundred is found who cherishes it in his heart, and not one in whom it grows to maturity so far is it from yielding fruit in its season.* Moreover, while some lose themselves in superstitious observances, and others, of set purpose, wickedly revolt from God, the result is that, in regard to the true knowledge of him, all are so degenerate, that in no part of the world can genuine godliness be found.[57] [emphasis mine]

As the Deer Pants

Now, many scientists will argue that there are scientific explanations for religious experiences—perhaps from evolutionary psychology or cognitive science. But do these accounts explain religious experience away? Remember, for one explanation to explain another away, the two must be

---

[56] "Not everyone who says to me, 'Lord, Lord,' will enter the kingdom of heaven, but only the one who does the will of my Father who is in heaven. Many will say to me on that day, 'Lord, Lord, did we not prophesy in your name and in your name drive out demons and in your name perform many miracles?' Then I will tell them plainly, 'I never knew you. Away from me, you evildoers!' (Matt. 7:21–23).

[57] John Calvin *Institutes*, 47 www.ccel.org/ccel/calvin/institutes.pdf

incompatible. However, it is not at all obvious that scientific explanations of religious experience are incompatible with theism. As philosopher Michael Murray argues:

> These models, if correct, show *not one thing more* than we have certain mental tools...which under certain conditions give rise to beliefs in the existence of entities which tend to rally religious commitments. But, pointing that out does nothing, all by itself, to tell us whether those beliefs are justified or not. After all, we have mental tools which, under certain conditions, give rise to belief in the existence of palm trees and electrons. We do not regard those belief-forming mechanisms as unreliable nor (typically) the beliefs formed as unjustified.[58]

The only question that we need ask is, 'Does the mechanism produce a true belief in the appropriate circumstances?' God has control over the course of nature and would have the ability to prime our nervous systems to react in certain ways in certain circumstances. If God directs nature, if nature gave us faculties that prompt us to believe in God's presence, and if God really is present, then our religious experiences are reliable. So a scientific explanation for religious experiences gives us no grounds to doubt that they tell the truth.

How do these various religious experiences provide evidence for God's existence? A good hypothesis should lead us to *expect observations that other hypotheses do not predict.* Alvin Plantinga points out that:

> The God of Theism would very likely desire that there be creatures who resemble him in being rational and intelligent; he would also, no doubt, desire that there be

---

[58]   Michael Murray, 'Scientific Explanations of Religion and the Justification of Religions Belief,' in *The Believing Primate: Scientific, Philosophical, and Theological Reflections on Evolutionary Explanations of Religion* Edited Michael Murray and Jeffrey Schloss (Oxford: 2010), 169

creatures who have a moral sense, and can tell right from wrong; and he would also very likely desire that there be creatures who can experience his presence and who are moved to worship by God's greatness and goodness.[59]

If there is no God, it is very surprising that conscious beings evolved in the first place, never mind conscious rational beings with religious beliefs, convictions and experiences.[60] Religious experience is neatly explained if God created human beings; if atheism is true, it is merely an odd and unexpected consequence of human evolution.

Theism also explains our *spiritual desires*. One example of a *spiritual desire* is our fierce desire for justice; another is our longing for forgiveness and mercy.[61] We cannot bear the thought of child-killers escaping without consequence. Yet if the just and the unjust are annihilated at their deaths, and if the universe is the pitiless and indifferent place that Dawkins describes, then justice is an impossibility. At the same time, we are keenly aware of the gap that exists between our behaviour and what morality demands. We sense the need for forgiveness.

There are other spiritual desires. We need providence: the reassurance that, whatever happens in an uncertain world, everything will eventually work out for the good. We yearn to know that we have eternal significance and meaning; that our lives amount to more than the few brief years that we live on earth. We want to experience awe; to feel dwarfed by experiences of majesty and wonder. We feel the call to be good; to be capable of genuine self-emptying love. Above all we ache

---

[59] Alvin Plantinga *Where the Conflict Really Lies* (Oxford: 2012), 52–53

[60] 'Evolutionary Accounts of Religion: Explaining and Explaining Away' by Michael Murray and Andrew Goldberg, and 'Explaining Religious Experience' by Charles Taliaferro, both in *The Believing Primate* (Schloss, Murray eds).

[61] My account of the 'spiritual desires' is based on Clifford Williams excellent *Existential Reasons for Belief in God* (IVP Academic: 2011).

to receive unlimited love; a love that comes without conditions and that never fails.

Interestingly, atheism does not seem able to satisfy or explain our spiritual desires. Bertrand Russell wrote:

> I believe that when I die I shall rot, and nothing of my ego will survive. I am not young, and I love life. But I should scorn to shiver with terror at the thought of annihilation. Happiness is none the less true happiness because it must come to an end, nor do thought and love lose their value because they are not everlasting.[62]

It is true that thought and love would not lose *all* their value if atheism is true; but they would lose the value that we demand. On atheism love is ephemeral; it supervenes on the nervous systems of machines that have been randomly selected to pass along genetic information. Humanity will pass away as the stars die. So it is *obviously true* that *eternal* love is more valuable than a fleeting, finite human love. Our craving for meaning and significance demands more than a finite love. We need everlasting love if we are to be of eternal consequence.

It is difficult to see why natural selection would favour spiritual desires. We could probably get along better without the need for everlasting love. So why do we feel these needs? Perhaps they are the unintended side effects of human neurology. Alvin Plantinga notes how one evolutionary psychologist uses this strategy to explain our love of beautiful music—'it just happens to tickle several important parts of the brain in a highly pleasurable way, as cheesecake tickles the palate.'[63] Perhaps our spiritual desires could be explained in the same way; perhaps, our brains just happen to be 'stimulated' by them.

But we require a better explanation than 'stuff just happens'! The spiritual desires require a satisfying explanation because

---

[62] Quoted by Richard Dawkins *The God Delusion*, 397
[63] Alvin Plantinga's *Where the Conflict Really Lies*, 132

they define human nature. Anyone who has felt them keenly will not be satisfied with attempts to explain them away. These desires recur in literature and mythology across different times and cultures, and depth psychologists from Freud to Adler to Becker attempted to give some account of them. They are not mere wishes: the desires for meaning, love and awe are *challenging*. If all our spiritual needs were met, we would undergo a painful, personal and moral transformation.

Theism satisfactorily explains our fundamental, spiritual needs; for only God can *at once* meet our need for awe and love, for providence, meaning and justice. Only a God of unlimited power and love could measure up to our demands. If atheism is true the spiritual desires are futile, an absurd and unexpected consequence of our evolutionary history. Whereas it would be much less surprising that humans have spiritual desires if theism was true. As CS Lewis famously argued

> Creatures are not born with desires unless satisfaction for these desires exists. A baby feels hunger; well, there is such a thing as food. A duckling wants to swim; well, there is such a thing as water. Men feel sexual desire; well, there is such a thing as sex. If I find in myself a desire which no experience in this world can satisfy, the most probable explanation is that I was made for another world.[64]

So theism explains humanity's religious desires. Even Richard Dawkins concedes the power of religious experience when he notes that 'it is entirely plausible that the strong arms of God, even if they are purely imaginary, could console in just the same way as the real arms of a friend.' Now the good professor does not think that this is a good reason to believe in God. After all, a terminally ill patient can be relieved by a misdiagnosis which tells them that they are on the road to recovery. False beliefs can provide comfort; that does not make them rational.

[64]   C. S. Lewis *Mere Christianity* (HarperCollins: 2001), 136–137

But when a bereaved parent is comforted by the strong arms of God, they are not merely being comforted by a *belief*. They are receiving *consolation* from a *person*. Many people have been comforted in just this way—in fact, a whole body of Christian literature is devoted to such experiences. And the experience of God is not merely a source of emotional comfort; many self-aware, intelligent and educated men and women have testified that the experience of God *consoled their spiritual desires*. Perhaps all these individuals have been deluded; but if so, nature has been set up to play some very cruel tricks on us.

So widespread religious experiences and human spiritual needs provide some intriguing evidence for the existence of God. But notice that we reached this conclusion as *outsiders*. We set our own experiences aside, and considered reports of religious experiences in a cool, detached manner. Whereas most believers are confirmed *insiders*—they believe on the basis of their own experience. Is this irrational?

Trinitarian Waterfalls and Other Experiences

Let's take a concrete example. Early in his medical career, the future head of the Human Genome Project, Dr Francis Collins, was challenged by a patient to examine the case for God's existence. Collins had been an atheist up to that point, but reckoned that a good scientist should be open to a variety of hypotheses. As he studied the evidence, he was impressed by the moral argument for God's existence and the evidence for Jesus' resurrection. He struggled to make up his mind—should he embrace Christianity, or remain a sceptic? A religious experience would eventually decide the issue for him:

> In a muddle about all of this, on a beautiful afternoon...
> I went hiking in the Cascade Mountains in the northwest
> of the United States. It was a sunny day, the sky was perfect-
> ly blue, and I had that experience that we are occasionally
> given of being cleared of all of the distractions that other-

wise get in the way of thinking about what really matters. I just left the car and walked up a hiking trail. I had no idea where I was, and it's a wonder I didn't get lost.

As I walked up that trail I turned a corner and there was a sheer cliff face in front of me, at the top of which there must have been a small trickle of moisture. As that trickle came down the cliff it froze, and glinting in the sun was this frozen waterfall that came down in three cascades. I'd never seen anything like this before. It would take anybody's breath away, spiritual or not, to see this beauty of nature. But it caught me at a moment where I realized that this was an opportunity to ask the question that we all have to ask at some point. Do I believe in God? Am I ready to say yes to that question?

And I found that all of my resistance fell away. Not in a way that I could tell you precisely, in terms of 'Yes, I went through this logical argument and that theorem.' No, it just was a sense of 'I am ready to give myself to the love that God represents and that has reached out to me. I am ready to put aside my resistance and become the believer that I think God wants me to be.'[65]

In many ways, this report is similar in form and content to many other religious experiences; this was an 'ordinary' theistic experience. Seemingly, Collins was overwhelmed by the sense that God was responsible for the beauty of nature. This is perfectly consistent with the Christian belief that God not only transcends the universe; God is also immanent in this universe, guiding it through his providence, and upholding its existence at every moment.

This experience was a tipping point for Collins; it was the final straw that pressed him to believe in God. The story was also the final straw for many of Collin's academic despisers. When Collins wrote about his religious experience in his

[65]   Francis Collins full testimony can be read at www.bethinking.org/science-christianity/test-of-faith-chapter-1-learning-the-language-of-god.pdf

popular book *The Language of God,* the journal 'Nature' took the opportunity to praise Collins for his work in Science and the Church. Sam Harris exploded in a letter to the editors

> ...What does the 'mode of thought' displayed by Collins have in common with science? *The Language of God* should have sparked gasping outrage from the editors at *Nature*. Instead, they deemed Collins's efforts 'moving' and 'laudable'[66]

Jerry Coyne worried that Collin's 'superstitions' might hinder scientific research[67]. Coyne insisted that there are no 'other ways of knowing' than science. But, as we have already noted, there isn't a single scientific theory that includes the proposition 'only believe in the findings of the physical sciences.' No scientific experiment ends with the result 'only science provides meaningful answers.' There is no *scientific* way of knowing that 'science is the only way of knowing'.

In fact, if science is 'the only way of knowing' we would have to ask Harris, Coyne and Myers why they write so many books and articles. We do not interpret another person's writing using Physics, Chemistry or Biology. We do not use mathematical models or rigorous experimentation. To interpret a writer we need imagination and intuition, empathy and experience. It is rather difficult to come up with a strict set of rules for interpretation; there is no algorithm for hermeneutics. Yet we all know that Dawkins did not write 'The God Delusion' to gain a Bishopric. So there is at least *one* way of knowing beyond the methods of science.

Science has an incredible track record for discovering the truth about the material world. But if Science answers *one kind of question*—questions about the nature of the physical world—

---

[66] www.nature.com/nature/journal/v448/n7156/full/448864a.html

[67] whyevolutionistrue.wordpress.com/2009/07/10/francis-collins-as-nih-director/ (retrieved 25 Feb 2012).

remarkably well, it does not follow that it will answer *every kind of question* remarkably well. It certainly doesn't follow that these are the only type of question worth asking. We are in danger of missing answers to questions about value, meaning and purpose if we restrict our evidence to the evidence provided by the physical sciences.

The Inside Story on Good and Evil

For example, most people believe that good and evil and beauty are as real as gravity and electromagnetism. We generally hold that some moral truths are not the accidental by-product of human psychology, but are real and important. Of course sceptics might attempt to explain away beliefs in such 'metaphysical realities.' But does anyone really believe that it isn't genuinely, objectively evil to torture a child to death for sadistic pleasure? Does anyone really believe that every new-born child is a monstrosity? Or that the crematoria of Auschwitz were wonderful and beautiful?

Corporal Anton Schmidt was stationed in the Lithuanian town of Vilna during 'Operation Barbarossa'—Hitler's invasion of the Soviet Union. There he witnessed the Lithuanian Militia execute over 2000 Jews. The children tried to grab onto tree trunks as they were dragged away. 'You know what I'm like, with my soft heart,' he later wrote to his wife 'I couldn't think, and then helped them.' Schmidt dedicated his life to saving as many Jews as he could. He hid survivors, and spirited them away to new homes. He forged false papers, and gave Jewish fugitives jobs in his truck repair yard. He invited the Jewish resistance to meet in his quarters. Over six months he saved dozens of lives.

But Schmidt does not seem to have been a natural 'double agent.' He took so many risks, and helped so many people, that he quickly came to the attention of the Gestapo. He was arrested in January 1942, and executed that April. 'Please forgive me,' he wrote to his wife and daughter 'I acted only as a human being, and never wanted to harm anyone.' Schmidt was not a cultured or highly educated man; he rarely read newspapers and never opened books. But he was driven by a profound motive. 'We are all human beings' was his constant refrain.

Compare Schmidt's simple compassion with the maxim that motivated Joseph Stalin 'To choose ones victims, to prepare ones plans minutely, to slake an implacable vengeance, and then to go to bed—there is nothing sweeter in the world.' Contrast Schmidt's actions to those of Alois Knabel, a soldier in the 8th SS Infantry Regiment. Knabel perfected the art of soothing very young children who were witnessing SS massacres. It made it easier for him to shoot them in the back of the neck[68].

It seems impossible to read these accounts and not believe that Schmidt's actions were genuinely and objectively good, and that Knabel's actions were genuinely and objectively evil. Any society that could 'invent' a list of rules that would justify Knabel and condemn Schmidt would be insane. Human life is too precious, and compassion is too delicate a commodity. We cannot understand the tragedies of the last century until we tear back our 'emotional curtains', and passionately engage with these stories. *Some knowledge is reserved for insiders.*

We can grant that some people are 'outsiders' to some moral feelings. They lack moral experiences like guilt or sympathy. Yet even an 'outsider' can be convinced that moral values are real, and are not human inventions. Sociopaths are the first to justify their actions; even if they lack moral feelings, they have clear concepts of right and wrong. They could be convinced of moral realities by the evidence from the social sciences. Although different cultures disagree about *moral rules*, every culture believes in *moral values* like compassion and honesty.

'Outsiders' to moral *feelings* could be convinced that there are objective moral truths. When all the evidence, psychological,

---

[68] Knabel and Schmidt appear in Michael Burleigh's *Moral Combat* (HarperPress: 2011).

sociological and philosophical, is amassed, it is easy to argue that real moral values exist. Even so, we would reckon that outsiders lack a full understanding of morality. Most people do not believe in the reality of beauty and goodness because they have worked through a philosophical proof; they believe because they are 'insiders' convinced by their own moral feelings that moral values are as real as any law or substance described by science.

My 'inside' experience of morality can justify my belief in some basic moral absolutes—the dignity of human life, say, or the value of compassion. Now, religious experiences are just as powerful as the experience of goodness, obligation and beauty. So, arguably, they carry the same justifying power *for the person who has the experience*. A sceptic might object that moral experiences are more widely reported than experiences of God. But God is not an impersonal rule or value; God is personal. So God can *choose* how and when to reveal himself; the theist will not be at all concerned if some people do not share her religious experiences. Some people lack a moral experience; that does not make it wise to disregard my own.

Of course our moral and religious experiences need to be evaluated. We should not endorse *uncritical* devotion to ideas based on *nothing more* than emotional experiences. If we believed that our emotions were being manipulated, or that we are emotionally imbalanced for other reasons, we should not trust any beliefs derived from our experiences. And if the beliefs that we form simply do not make sense, given what we know about the world and about ourselves, we should reject them. With this in mind, we can ask if Dr Francis Collins' was irrational to accept God's existence on the basis of his waterfall experience—his 'insider test'.

Dr Collins was in good mental health, and he had his religious experience while hiking in the wilderness; he was hardly vulnerable to psychological manipulation at the time. His religious experience was not atypical; nor did it imply an irrational set of beliefs. For example, he did not hear a voice telling him that a perfectly loving God wanted him to kill as many innocents as possible. If that had been the case, Collins could have dismissed the very idea as incoherent and meaningless. So Dr Collins had no good reason to doubt his experience.

Crucially, Collins' new belief in God not only made sense of his religious experience; it helped him to make sense of his entire world. He could see that the evidence of morality did not undermine, but strengthened, the *experiential evidence* that he gained from his own personal experience of God. When he looked at all the evidence available to him, he did not find anything that undermined his religious experience. And the best explanation for all of his evidence, the objective evidence available to everyone, and his own private 'insider' experience, was that God is real.

The 'Outsider Test' asks if Christianity can provide an explanation for the world around us. The evidence of design, morality and the resurrection of Jesus mean that the Christian faith passes that test superlatively. The 'Insider Test' asks if Christian theism coheres with our inner experiences. We argued that spiritual desires and religious experiences can give us good reason to believe in God. However, as we will see, only the gospel reveals a God worthy of worship; without the cross and resurrection of Jesus our spiritual desires could never be sated.

A Gospel for Good Men and Scoundrels

"How do you know all this?," he cried. "Are you a devil?"
"I am a man," answered Father Brown gravely; "and
therefore have all devils in my heart."
G. K. Chesterton, *The Honour of Israel Gow*

For the message of the cross is foolishness to those who
are perishing, but to us who are being saved it is the power
of God.

The New Atheism represents a significant re-branding of
unbelief. Once upon a time, some atheists (the continental,
existential type) were angry at God for not existing; God's
absence robbed our world of significance. Marxists rejected
the Kingdom of God for a monumental struggle with history.
And nearly all atheists were outraged at the terrible suffering of
our world. Schopenhauer, for example, wished that the earth
had remained as lifeless as the moon. These atheists argued
that a good God would never have allowed such a world. This
'problem of evil' was the bedrock of Atheism.

But a gloomy demeanour doesn't suit the modern market-
place. A makeover was necessary if religion was to be challenged

as a source of meaning and hope. Some sceptics even took to calling themselves 'Brights'; no sense of despair there, then. If God doesn't exist, we should just look at the bright side of life; at least we can choose our own values. New Atheists are wild and witty, in a Python-esque way. They would rather write worship songs for a Flying Spaghetti Monster than engage with existential angst. This cheerful, cheeky nihilism has been popularised, mass produced and distributed at little cost to the consumer. The New Atheism might not be deep, but it is fun!

Yet we must respond to the problem of evil because it presents the greatest challenge to theism. Why would a perfect being, a personal God of unlimited love and power, create a world with suffering in it? The theist can give a neat, snappy reply to this question. God permits evil and suffering to bring about some greater good. Suffering provides us with the opportunity to grow in sympathy and compassion. God gave us the gift of moral responsibility; we chose to abuse that gift with cruelty and savagery. However, God can use pain to call us back to him, and to teach us to depend on him.

So there are greater goods, like moral responsibility and compassion, which justify the existence of evil. If only the problem of evil could be dodged so easily! There is so much suffering in the world; is it all necessary to bring these greater goods about? This is the problem of *gratuitous suffering*—some suffering seems to serve no greater good at all. Human responsibility does not require the existence of cancer or rabies. An anonymous, orphaned child dying unnoticed in a gutter allows no opportunity for compassion. Why doesn't God intervene to root this needless suffering out of the world?

The problem of *gratuitous suffering* is compounded by the problem of *horrendous evil*. Horrendous evils are so terrible that those who suffer them would rather not have been born. A parent who accidentally kills their own child and a child who has been raped repeatedly by their own parent have both suffered horrendous evils. A God of unlimited love would not just value human race as a whole; he would value each individual human being. He would want every human's life to have more good than evil in it; the problem of horrendous evils presents us with individual lives that seem to contain more evil than good.

So how can the Christian respond? By immediately pointing out that God did not create a world in which individuals, *through no fault of their own*, undergo lives which contain more evil than good. But we must remind the atheist that, if theism is true, the possibilities for goodness are not exhausted by what we observe in the world around us. God would be capable of sustaining a person in an afterlife, and a life of eternal bliss would outweigh any horrendous suffering that we have experienced here.

So a theist could respond to the problem of *horrendous evils* by insisting that God can overwhelm evil with good in the New Creation. God will allow no-one to undergo a life with more torment than blessing *unless they reject the blessing on offer.*[69] What about the problem of gratuitous suffering? Many evils do not seem to directly bring about some greater good. So, some theists concede that many tragedies do not increase the amount of goodness in the universe; if God brought a 'greater good' by allowing Alois Knabel to shoot children in the neck, then only He knows what it is.

However, God *offers* every human an eternal life good enough to overwhelm any amount of suffering. Furthermore, God guarantees that evil will not have the final say; God's victory is assured. So, these theists argue, why should we expect God to prevent every instance of gratuitous suffering? God would be forced to intervene continuously in our world, changing

---

[69] There is not the slightest doubt in my mind that Hell is a real and present danger for human beings. We are damaged and dangerous creatures who would willingly forgo an eternity of blessing if it kept us free from God's love. See www.saintsandsceptics.org/is-hell-hot-in-hollywood/

the nature of our universe, and seriously undermining human responsibility. Gratuitous evils might just be the price we pay to have moral responsibility.[70]

Other theists are not comfortable with this answer; they are inclined to think that God ordained *all things* for the good.[71] They point out that humans need to remember their limitations when thinking about God and suffering. Consider insects so small that they are invisible to the naked human eye. If an entomologist were to tell you that your arm was covered in such insects, it would not be rational to deny this because you cannot see any insects. You are not in a position to detect these creatures with your eyes.

So consider the gap between God's mind and ours. We should concede we are not in a position to detect all the goods that God knows of. True, we cannot understand what possible good could come from the actions of murderous Nazis; it seems as if the world would have been better off without them. However, God's purposes will be infinitely more subtle than we can imagine; his capacity to bring good out of suffering will surpass all human knowledge.

The different theistic responses to the problem of evil sounds like great theories, but they are hardly sources of great comfort. We have established that evil does not provide decisive counter-evidence to theism; but we have been forced to admit that some of it *seems* gratuitous. We do not have a neat, tidy explanation for many terrible events. And, in any case, those

---

[70] Peter Van Inwagen 'The Problem of Evil' in Wainwright ed. *The Oxford Handbook of the Philosophy of Religion* (Oxford: 2005); Thomas F. Tracy 'Victimization and the Problem of Evil: A Response to Ivan Karamazov' *Faith and Philosophy* 1992, 9:3) 301-319.

[71] Chad Meister *Evil: A Guide for the Perplexed* (Continuum: 2012); Stephen J. Wykstra 'The Human obstacle to evidential arguments from suffering: On avoiding the evils of "appearance"' *International Journal for Philosophy of Religion* 16 (2):73–93 (1984).

who have suffered horrendous evils are rarely interested in the implications for philosophy of religion.

Yet, if the Christian cannot supply a complete explanation of evil, she *can provide a reason to trust God.* The Son of God was crucified for us; and the Father's heart was broken. The message of the cross includes the revelation that God has suffered for us and with us. In fact, if God turned his face away from his son in anger (as Jesus' cry 'Why have you forsaken me?' indicates) then God has suffered more than we ever could. The cross is a sign that God's love, and God's mercy, dwarfs all imagination.

It is also a sign that God's goodness will overwhelm suffering. On the first Good Friday, Jesus' disciples would have believed that God had abandoned his Messiah. That belief would have needed an urgent reassessment in the light of Easter Morning. The Father did not forsake the Son, and God will not forsake us. The Christian might not have neat explanations for every instance of suffering; but the cross and the resurrection provide the Christian with reasons to trust God. And these are not events that have occurred in an abstract, metaphysical realm. They are part of our history, concrete examples of God's goodness.

In the last chapter we pointed out that humans have a need for consolation; we all have fundamental spiritual needs that define us. One of those needs is the need for salvation. We need to know that our suffering matters; that it is not the contingent side effect of evolutionary history. We need to know that there is a way out of suffering; not by pretending that suffering is an illusion, but knowing that one day suffering will be defeated. The message of the cross provides the consolation that we need in the presence of evil. And this message is not mere wish fulfilment; it is confirmed by the resurrection of Jesus.

But the cross and the resurrection were not just intended to bring an end to the unrelenting chaos in the world around us; the message of the cross is that God's son died to end the bedlam that rules in each human heart. This is an offensive message;

we do not wish to acknowledge that we are so flawed that only the death of the Son of God could heal us. Nevertheless, the message of the cross, and God's call to be transformed by it, is the final piece of evidence that we want to consider.

The Story So Far...

Let's take a breath and rehearse what I have argued so far. Christians believe in a personal God of limitless loving power. Theism can be treated as a hypothesis, and we can find evidence that supports this hypothesis. If there are features of the universe that reflect purpose, a personal God would explain those features; we would have evidence of God's existence. The universe's order and structure, objective moral values, the resurrection of Jesus Christ and human spiritual needs are all ultimately explained by theism.

We have also noted that a person can have reliable *personal, experiential* evidence of God's existence. Now, intellectuals from Plato to Kurt Godel have found the case for God to be intellectually interesting and compelling. But a theoretical belief in God's existence is of little value if it is not accompanied with a personal trust in God. A God of love would not be interested in the speculations of life's spectators. It is important to know *that* God exists. It is also good to know *what* God is—unlimited power and love. But we should not be satisfied until we know *who* God is.

If theism is true, it does not merely *describe* the universe. Theism also *prescribes* how we should live. If God is the Perfect Being then *nothing else is more worthy of worship!* It follows that we should seek to worship God; we should want to know God, and to be transformed by him. This gives us a way to assess the credibility of the Christian gospel, for any true revelation should describe an unsurpassable God, more worthy of worship than anything else that we can imagine. Furthermore, any true revelation should seek to challenge us, transform us, and answer our deepest needs.

As we noted at the end of chapter 5, Christianity reveals that God is Father, Son and Holy Spirit, three persons, inextricably linked by the same unlimited power and love. God the Father gave his only Son, who suffered and died for us. The love of God stretches our imaginations and conceptions to breaking point. Who else could be worthy of worship? Furthermore, the gospel of Jesus Christ is challenging and consoling in equal measure. It reassures us that God is with us and for us; but it also demands that we unconditionally surrender to the love of God in faith and repentance.

We tend to associate worship with any activity performed in a church, or our acts of religious observance. We might not understand Christian rituals; we often have no emotional connection with them. Still, we tend to act as if worship consists of taking bread and wine at the right time in the right way and repeating the right lines from the right prayer. Or, if we attend a Church with a 'user-friendly service', we might identify worship with brief, intense experiences generated by the enthusiasm of a band of contemporary musicians.

To identify religious experiences, however profound, or religious observance as *true worship* is to get the cart before the horse. We might well experience transcendence or awe; we might have a keen sense of God's providential care. But compared to true worship such religious experiences are worthless. If God is truly worthy of worship—if he is as good as it gets—then worshipping him will cost us our mind, soul, will and understanding. Simply put, it means allowing God to have the final say over everything that we are.

That is to say, *true worship* begins with a changed heart. Before our acts of worship can mean anything at all we must trust God, asking him to change our characters, our motivations and our desires. The process might be sudden and dramatic; it might be subtle and gradual. But unless we allow God to occupy our hearts, to dominate and exploit our emotions and desires for his own ends, we simply are not worshipping him. We have not realised who or what God is.

Homer Simpson's Heresy

But this all sounds rather melodramatic; isn't this the sort of guilt trip that a revivalist preacher uses to boost Church attendance? This brings us to the heresy of Homer Simpson. Not too long into the life of *The Simpsons*, Homer discovered that skipping Church on a Sunday morning can be an incredibly liberating experience.[72] (Unless you have experienced weekly Church attendance as a mere mandatory religious duty, you cannot even begin to imagine Homer's sense of emancipation. I imagine that the French felt something similar on D-Day.)

In and of itself, skipping one Church service would be of little consequence. This wasn't even an act of religious defiance; Homer simply wanted a moment's freedom from life's dull routine. But then Homer reasoned that Church attendance should be optional for the religious man. He declared that he would never attend Church again. He would worship God in his own way, largely by doing whatever he wanted on a Sunday morning. Thankfully, Homer's evangelical neighbour, some cute ducks, and a Jewish clown intervened to restore Homer's faith. (Well, they persuaded him to attend church again.)

Homer never really lost whatever 'faith' he had; he simply wanted free time on Sunday mornings to watch sports. As a heretic Homer was a spectacular failure; but his argument for abandoning Church must have resonated with many viewers: 'I'm not a bad guy, I work hard, and I love my kids...so why should I spend half my Sunday hearing about how I'm going to hell?' Granted, Homer's comic selfishness might not make him the best person to advance the argument. But surely *we're* decent people. We do our best to do what's right. We care for our families and friends. So isn't it excessive to insist that every

[72] 'Homer the Heretic', *The Simpsons*, Season 4 Episode 3, first aired 8 Oct 1992.

human being must capitulate to God? Surely a God of love couldn't demand anything like our unconditional surrender?

The problem with this objection is that it misunderstands the nature of love. We tend to view love as a desire or a feeling; and love is never *less than* an emotional experience. But love is much *more than* an emotion. We only love when we value another's happiness more than we value our own. We cannot tell if we love someone by examining our feelings for them; we tell how much we love another by asking what we would sacrifice for them. If God wants us to truly love him, he might ask us to sacrifice quite a bit. After all, he has made an unimaginable sacrifice for us; God the Son died to pay our debt.

But this takes us back to Homer's original objection. If we're doing our best, and don't go out of our way to hurt others, why do we need to hear all this talk of forgiveness and atonement? It all seems terribly old fashioned and archaic. We didn't ask for Jesus' sacrifice, and it doesn't seem that we needed it. Couldn't God just accept us for who we are? Do we have to return to this repressive and restrictive talk about human sinfulness?

Christianity is offensive because it does not teach that 'humanity is good'. Christians believe that man is a ruined masterpiece, 'a good being gone bad.' We were made in God's image, but we have chosen to bury his likeness deep in the darkness; we only feel its influence when we find it convenient. So we need to pay attention to some inconvenient truths about ourselves; we need to stare into the abyss in our hearts.

Sins and Misdemeanours

G. K. Chesterton reminds us that when men stop believing in God, they will believe in any absurdity. The secular world insists that we are not sinners; that we should think of ourselves as innately good and worthy individuals. We would be more comfortable believing that the doctrine of sin is a relic of Europe's unenlightened and repressive past. But history, philosophy and art remind us that this is a blind, irrational and dangerous belief. As Chesterton puts it:

> If it be true (as it certainly is) that a man can feel exquisite happiness in skinning a cat, then the religious philosopher can only draw one of two deductions. He must either deny the existence of God, as all atheists do; or he must deny the present union between God and man, as all Christians do. The new theologians seem to think it a highly rationalistic solution to deny the cat.[73]

Of course most teenagers do not enjoy skinning cats; they would rather watch films. Which brings us to the most offensive aspect of the doctrine of sin—it is much too egalitarian. It puts the label 'wicked' on every human being regardless of class, colour or creed. It would be more convenient to divide the world into 'evil' men (like terrorists and paedophiles) and the rest of us. The deeds of evil people are incomprehensible and inexcusable; our misdeeds are mere misfortunes. Evil men must be eradicated; we who remain must learn to forgive ourselves.

J. R. R. Tolkien followed Plato's parable of the Ring to illuminate our hidden depths. Both writers asked us to imagine a ring that rendered its owner invisible; then they asked us to consider what effect the ring would have on its bearer. A new world of possibilities opened up for the man who owned such a ring. In an age before forensic science, the owner of the ring could do what he pleased, when he pleased, without fear of prosecution. The law could not punish him; he would not even have to worry about his public reputation. He could take what he desired when he desired it.

And what effect would this power have on a human? He might start with petty acts of revenge, and little acts of theft. But he could act on every impulse for revenge, sate every appetite, and not have to worry about the consequences. How

---

[73] *Orthodoxy* (Moody Press:2009), 28.

long could he resist the temptation to do terrible things to those who had wronged him? How long before he sought out every forbidden fruit? The parable of the ring reveals that there is a terrible desire for power, and a lust for experience, in each human psyche. We need the fear of retribution, and the desire for a good reputation, to keep our darker nature in check.

History confirms the results of this thought experiment. When attempting to discover why the great atrocities of the last century occurred, agnostic philosopher Jonathan Glover discovered that many ordinary men and women were capable of the most terrible crimes when they knew that there would be no consequence for their actions. Conscripts were transported to the other side of the globe to face enemies for whom they had no empathy, in a place where no moral authority reigned. The result was atrocity on an unimaginable scale.[74]

Every day we inflict dozens of little acts of cruelty on our neighbours; we express our selfishness every hour that we live. There is a gap between the good that we know we ought to do, and what we achieve. We bear responsibility for the shortfall. This is not a counsel of despair. It is a plea for self-knowledge and wisdom; it is an attempt to illuminate the gulf between God and humanity. If we cannot see our need for redemption then the message of the cross will make little sense to us.

Try another thought experiment. In the film 'The Final Cut' scientists known as Cutter's can implant a recording device in a person's brain at birth. This device will create an audio-visual recording of their every conscious moment. When they die, a Cutter will select 'scenes' from their consciousness, the most significant moments of your life, and turn these into a film that sums up their identity. The film will be shown at their funeral—a 'Re-memory.' This becomes a focus for the grieving family, a reassurance that the deceased's life had significance.

---

[74] Jonathan Glover, *Humanity: a moral history of the Twentieth Century* (Pimilico: 2001).

Of course the Cutter 'edits out' any details that will shock or offend mourners and retains a few moments of sentimental value. For our thought experiment, reverse the premise of the film. Imagine that a cutter has recorded your every conscious moment, but will only create a film from the moments you are most ashamed of. Make a quick mental list of what this will include. The list will include every time you have spoken ill of someone who loves you. It will include every time that you have *thought* ill of someone who loves you, or when wished that you could betray them. It will include every cruel ambition and vengeful fantasy.

Could you bear to be in the room with your family while this film played? Could you let them know what you have said and thought about them all? Or would you rather disappear into a mouse-hole than face what you actually are? And here's the rub: this is exactly the position we *all* find ourselves in once we acknowledge that there is a God. God, by definition, is perfectly good and knows every truth. He knows us better than we know ourselves. How could you bear to be known by a perfect God; one who knows exactly which rules you have willingly broken? Who knows what we would do if we could escape the consequences...

We are drawn to the holiness of God; only his unlimited, loving power can satiate the hunger in our souls. However, we are not holy. We are not pure enough to draw near to God, because his knowledge would expose us for what we are. This is the human problem: we are drawn to the light of God's holiness, only to discover it is like an all-consuming fire. We cover our shame by retreating to the shadows, only to find that we are miserable once more. If only someone could take the shame away; if only something could make us holy as God is holy.

What about the good that we do? Isn't that enough to atone for our failures? Unfortunately, that seems doubtful. God made us to be good. I like it that my car starts when I turn the key in the morning. That's what it was made to do. If it fails to start four or five mornings out of ten, then the other mornings that it did manage to start will be of little consolation to me. I expect my car to do what it was made to do all the time. The same standard applies to humans. We were made to be good. It's pleasing to God, presumably, when we choose to do what is right. But we are hardly doing him a favour—working up extra merit as it were. This is just what God should expect from us.

So we cannot change ourselves to be suitable for a deep, intimate relationship with God. We need God to provide the means; this is what God's Son did on the cross. He took the punishment we deserved and suffered the shame of our fall. Of course, it's reasonable to ask how the suffering of the Son of God can benefit us. The answer is that it can't—*unless we choose to identify ourselves with Jesus*. We identify ourselves with other people all the time by forming unions with them. For example, we marry, we take children into our families, and we transfer citizenship from one nation to another.

When we do these things we change who we are. Our identity becomes inextricably linked with the identities of our new family members, or with history of our new country. We must take some responsibility for the other individuals in the 'team' that we join—just as they take some responsibility for us. Philosopher John Hare asks us to

> ...consider marriage. How is it that I can be ashamed or proud of what my wife does, and she can be ashamed or proud of what I do? When she does well at an interview and gets the job she wants, I am pleased and proud for her. But the truth is also expressed by saying that she and I together form a unit, and I am pleased and proud for the both of us. It is true that I may also feel envy and resentment, and gird myself for new battles about the division of responsibilities. But if the marriage is functioning well, you might see a new spring in my stride, a greater sense of self-confidence, that would be altogether mysterious if we could not understand the transfer or transmission of pride within the unit.

> Similarly if I fail in some disastrous way at work, especially if it seems that the whole world knows about it, my wife and I will both be dragged down by it. It is not just that she feels sympathy for me in my predicament. It is that she has been humiliated together with me, and we will both feel the urge to hide from public view. This kind of example can be extended ... into relations of close friendship, and beyond that into relations of collegiality at work, and so on.[75]

We form alliances and unions all the time. When we do, we can take responsibility for one another's failings and credit for each other's achievements. This helps us to understand the cross. We need no longer fear God's judgment if we are identified with Christ. Jesus paid the price of our disgrace. He took responsibility for our faults. If we are united with God's Son, and he takes possession of us as his rightful property, *he* takes the consequences of our failures. He covers our shame; we need no longer feel the pain of our moral and spiritual flaws. Christ raises us up, as one of his own. If he did not, an eternal relationship with God would be too painful for us to bear.

A union with the Son of God would be more demanding than any human relationship. It would mean acknowledging Christ as sovereign, giving him complete rights over our characters and our minds. This is challenging. But God would want to challenge us morally—and more than morally. God would want to challenge us on every level of our being; so God calls us to the cross. This evidence does not come in the form of detached, objective observations, that every competent observer can acknowledge. This evidence is *personal*. We can feel it working *directly* on our conscience as God calls us to surrender to him.

Sneers at the Cross

Christianity is not just a set of truths about the Father, Son

---

[75] www.calvin.edu/academic/philosophy/writings/moralato.htm. Hare gives a convincing explanation of sin and atonement in *The Moral Gap* (Oxford: 1997).

and Holy Spirit; it is a call to know God personally, and to be transformed by him. We can experience the power of this call in at least two ways. We can be morally challenged when we realise we are not morally fit for a relationship with God, and therefore desperately need the atonement provided by Christ. Or we can be emotionally challenged by God's perfect, sacrificial love.

The call to be transformed through Christ is a compelling experience that needs an explanation. Accepting the call is a source of consolation; the cross meets our needs for love, forgiveness, justice and hope. Crucially, Christian doctrine explains more than our inner, experiential evidence. The evidence provided by the universe's order and structure, by the reality of moral values and obligations, and for the Resurrection of Jesus Christ, verifies that Christianity is true. The end result is a powerful cumulative case for the truth of the gospel.

Yet, the Christian is not on a quest for intellectual respectability. Belief in God is worthless if we believe as one believes in an academic theory. *Knowing that* there is a God helps in the search for wisdom; *knowing God personally* saves a person from guilt and emptiness. To know God fully we have to travel to a cross, and accept that the life and death of the son of a Palestinian carpenter is the most important event in history. We need to believe that a Galilean teacher rose from the dead and triumphed over evil. For God became one of us in the most unassuming of places.

This message is not a neat academic theory; it will always have its cultured and educated despisers. But God's concern is not to bring our data bases up to speed. If Christianity is true, God's concern is to know us, to save us and to transform us. The sneers of culturally respectable academics are to be expected and, to some extent, welcomed. They remind us that the gospel is not merely a source of propositional knowledge; it is the way to know God. And the Christian can be confident that his God is not a delusion; for only at Calvary can we finally make sense of everything else that we know.

Why I Am Not An Atheist
Facing the Inadequacies of Unbelief
David J Randall

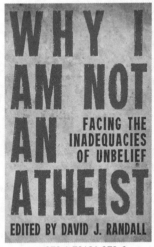

ISBN 978-1-78191-270-6

Eleven Christians – including a biologist, a psychiatrist, a journalist, and a debater – came on 11 different paths to God. How and why? This book is the compilation of their answers and experiences written in response to Bertrand Russell's *Why I Am Not A Christian*.

The authors faithfully fulfill the apostle Peter's exhortation to give the reason for the hope that they have in Christ.

James Anderson
Associate Professor of Theology, Reformed Theological Seminary, Charlotte, North Carolina

For the many honest, open-minded sceptics who do want to reasonably weigh all the evidence, this book will be thought-provoking, stimulating and perhaps even life-changing.

William Philip
Minister, The Tron Church, Glasgow

Contributors include Donald Bruce, Alistair Donald, Henk Drost, Elaine Duncan, Alex MacDonald, Pablo Martinez, David Randall, David Robertson, Chris Sinkinson, Heather Tomlinson and Ravi Zacharias.

Dawkins Letters
Challenging Atheist Myths
DAVID ROBERTSON

THE DAWKINS LETTERS
CHALLENGING ATHEIST MYTHS **DAVID ROBERTSON**

ISBN 978-1-84550-597-4

When Richard Dawkins published *The God Delusion*, David Robertson wanted an intelligent Christian response – and so he wrote it. This honest book draws on Robertson's experience as a debater, letter writer, pastor and author to clarify the questions and the answers for thinkers and seekers, and to respond to Dawkins in a gentle spirit of enquiry.

Wow, this is an intelligent and well-crafted view of RD's book.

> Response from an atheist
> on Richard Dawkins Website

The book does a particularly good job of point out the unending contradictions between what Dawkins wants to believe and what he must actually believe.

> Tim Challies
> Blogger at www.challies.com

David Robertson, author of *The Dawkins Letters* and *Awakening*, is pastor of St Peter's Free Church of Scotland. Robertson is a trustee of the Solas Centre for Public Christianity and works to fulfill the Centre's mission to engage culture with the message of Christ.

Christian Focus Publications

Our mission statement –

STAYING FAITHFUL
In dependence upon God we seek to impact the world through literature faithful to His infallible Word, the Bible. Our aim is to ensure that the Lord Jesus Christ is presented as the only hope to obtain forgiveness of sin, live a useful life and look forward to heaven with Him.

Our Books are published in four imprints:

CHRISTIAN FOCUS

popular works including biographies, commentaries, basic doctrine and Christian living.

CHRISTIAN HERITAGE

books representing some of the best material from the rich heritage of the church.

MENTOR

books written at a level suitable for Bible College and seminary students, pastors, and other serious readers. The imprint includes commentaries, doctrinal studies, examination of current issues and church history.

CF4•K

children's books for quality Bible teaching and for all age groups: Sunday school curriculum, puzzle and activity books; personal and family devotional titles, biographies and inspirational stories – because you are never too young to know Jesus!

Christian Focus Publications Ltd,
Geanies House, Fearn, Ross-shire,
IV20 1TW, Scotland, United Kingdom.
www.christianfocus.com